Promoting Positive Behaviour

Tim O'Brien

David Fulton Publishers

David Fulton Publishers Ltd
The Chiswick Centre, 414 Chiswick High Road, London W4 5TF
www.fultonpublishers.co.uk

First published in Great Britain in 1998 by David Fulton Publishers

Note: The rights of Tim O'Brien to be identified as the authors of this work
have been asserted by them in accordance with the Copyright, Designs and
Patents Act 1988.

David Fulton Publishers is a division of Granada Learning Limited, part of
Granada plc.

British Library Cataloguing in Publication Data
A catalogue record for this book is available from the British Library.

ISBN 1-85346-502-X

Typeset by Sheila Knight, London
Printed and bound in Great Britain

Contents

This book is dedicated to my parents Mary and Paddy

Foreword

'Behaviour', and all of its associated negative connotations, is the most common topic of conversation in staffrooms across the United Kingdom. In fact, internationally, many developed countries would report an ever-increasing number of children with disturbing behaviour patterns in their schools, and consequently growing levels of exclusions – what the Americans term, 'kids out of the system'.

Does our talk about the characteristics of the behaviour of these children include thoughts about their learning? Fundamentally, however challenging a child's behaviour may be in the context of the classroom, they do not sacrifice their entitlement to be regarded as, first and foremost, a learner. So what is this pupil group telling us about their curriculum – the diet of learning experiences offered to them?

Clearly, some are experiencing disenfranchisement from the curriculum; for them the curriculum does not offer that key curriculum tenet of the 1988 Education Reform Act – relevance. Rather it offers alienation; for a variety of reasons, some children find themselves on the periphery of the learning experience. Many of the behavioural traits that they choose to display are confrontational, and often offensive, towards the teacher. The natural human response from the teacher is to try to control the behaviour. In fact, what may be needed is further differentiation of 'the learning': an in-depth consideration of how lessons may be designed to penetrate the facade of difficult behaviour, and touch the child at their point of learning.

Teachers rightly feel challenged by this pupil group, and express concerns about the cost to other pupils in their classes of persistent and disruptive behaviour. *Promoting Positive Behaviour* seeks to refocus the debate on behaviour management (a term this book challenges) so that the individual is seen within the context of the wider school community, its ethos and the curricular context in which learning for all pupils takes place.

The Government Green paper (1997) on special educational needs recognises the problems that exist for schools in the complex area of emotional and behavioural difficulties and has made a commitment to working with teachers and schools to resolve some of these issues. Central to the Green Paper is its intention to promote inclusion in schools. This pupil group presents the biggest threat to inclusion. Their challenging behaviour disorientates the process of teaching and learning in the classroom leaving them (and sometimes their peers) with a set of fragmented learning experiences, lacking in coherence.

How *do* we build an inclusive curriculum and one that offers active participation to all pupils? The reported growth of provision for pupils with emotional and behavioural difficulties is testimony to our inability to design the curriculum in such a way that it is responsive to highly specific individual needs, as well as those in common with others.

Promoting Positive Behaviour offers new and creative insights into the teaching and learning of all pupils, but particularly those with behavioural difficulties. It powerfully reminds us that, through high quality learning, we can encourage pupils to exercise personal control of their own behaviour.

Socially unacceptable behaviours are likely to lead to avoidance and exclusion from local communities. Inclusion at societal level has to be the ultimate goal of educational forms of inclusion. The school is one community, but there is a wider community from which young people displaying unacceptable behaviours may find themselves excluded. We are charged with ensuring that this group of pupils do not risk losing their citizenship in their society as a result of inappropriate behaviours. After all, they are 'children first'.

Promoting Positive Behaviour challenges some of our value-laden thinking about pupils with needs in the area of behaviour. It displays the access routes to learning that are available through effective teaching and advocates a school ethos that engenders self-respect, mutual respect and dignity for all.

Barry Carpenter
Chief Executive, Sunfield, Clent, Worcestershire

Acknowledgements

I am grateful to Barry Carpenter for inviting me to take up a full-time secondment for 1997/1998 as a senior lecturer at the Centre for the Study of Special Education (CSSE) at Westminster College, Oxford. It is a pleasure to work with the dedicated CSSE team. The secondment has afforded me the privilege of working with pupils and teachers in many special and mainstream schools across the breadth of the country. It also provides an opportunity for me to become involved in initial teacher education. I would like to thank Dennis Goldthorpe and the governing body of Alexandra School for supporting the secondment. I thank my colleagues at Alexandra for the way in which they have always placed the needs of the children at the top of their priority list. I would also like to thank the pupils for moments of professional challenge and moments of great fun too. I am grateful to each individual that I have taught in special and mainstream settings for what they have taught me in return.

I would like to thank Professor Brahm Norwich – a joint illustration, from a recent discussion that we had together, appears as a figure in this book. Thanks to Carol Ouvry for agreeing that our differentiation model could appear in this text. I am grateful to Bryony Williamson, Jo Egerton, Dennis Guiney and Tony Warren for their helpful comments on the final draft of specific chapters. I would also like to say 'go raibh mile maith agat' to Sean McTernan. My list of acknowledgements would not be complete without thanking Paddy and Mary, Kevin, Cathy, Liz and Matthew.

A certain philosopher once claimed that there was only one thing in life that could not be retrieved – the missed opportunity. I would like to thank David Fulton Publishers for providing the prestigious 'Fulton Fellowship' and the colleagues who encouraged me to apply for it. I am pleased that I did not miss the opportunity to write *Promoting Positive Behaviour*. It was written as a result of being awarded the 1997/1998 Fulton Fellowship in Special Education.

Chapter 1

Behaviour and learning: the reunion

Introduction

Promoting positive behaviour can only occur in a mutually responsive learning environment that offers whole learning to a whole child within a whole school. This book provides a practitioner's perspective on how schools can promote positive behaviour among those pupils who experience learning difficulties and present challenging behaviour. It places a focus upon the learning needs of such children in a climate where the separation of behaviour and learning has begun to limit their opportunities for spiritual, moral, social and cultural development. The spiritual context of a child, within the curriculum and beyond it, is considered.

The book presents an argument that teachers need to define and observe behaviour so that they can understand it and change it for the better. Suggestions on how this might be done are offered within a context that considers the working reality of the classroom.

This book also details strategies and approaches for promoting positive behaviour so that teachers and pupils can stay in a learning zone and keep out of the battle zone. Finally, the book highlights the needs of staff who adopt a consistently positive approach in a potentially stressful working environment – teachers have needs too. This book reflects the eclectic nature of education and has one major aim – to improve the quality of teaching and learning for those children who find learning a challenge.

Current labels and special education

The world of education overflows with labels, categories and underlying assumptions. Schools, teachers, the curriculum, and the pupils are all subject to the institutionalisation of value-laden labels. Much of the content of this book is relevant to the common needs of every child who is in the education system. However, some emphasis has been placed on those whose learning needs have resulted in their being given some type of 'special' label. Owing to the significant learning difficulties that they experience, however relative this definition might be, these children are educated in 'special' schools while the majority of the population are educated within a setting that is described as 'mainstream'. Mainstream schools are also referred to as 'ordinary' schools. The polarisation of 'special' and 'ordinary' schools can emphasise the individual differences between children in a discriminatory manner. The international drive towards an inclusive educational system refers to 'regular' schools with an inclusive orientation (UNESCO 1994). Does this make those children who may need separate and distinct curricular provision 'irregular'?

The values and assumptions that are attached to labels will always be contentious in the field of special needs education. We have progressed from the days of children being labelled as having 'disabilities of body and mind' or being 'defective', 'subnormal', maladjusted', 'retarded' or 'backward' (Wedell 1990). Concerns now need to be raised about the inherent assumptions and status implications associated with the current labelling of 'special' schools and 'special' children. My concern begins with the national categorisation of special schools. If we are to assume that the category of the school functions as a descriptor of the children it teaches, then our current special school categories place an emphasis upon the *difficulties* that the children experience rather their learning *needs*. This emphasis can promote philosophical and pedagogical approaches that serve to create a culture where children with learning difficulties are seen as difficult and the task of teaching them, particularly if their learning need presents as a 'behaviour difficulty', is seen in a similarly negative fashion.

What assumptions are we to make about those children who attend a school which caters for 'Severe Learning Difficulties' (SLD), a school for 'Moderate Learning Difficulties' (MLD) or one for 'Emotional and Behavioural Difficulties' (EBD)? In each of these three categories of special school, the emphasis is placed on the difficulties that the children bring to the school environment. Such a focus places a barrier to understanding and catering for the needs of each child. New Labour entered government with three main priorities – 'education, education and education'. This positive and commendable commitment to education for all does not sit comfortably next to a special school perspective of 'difficulties, difficulties and difficulties'. The emphasis on difficulties must alter so that we can begin to reflect the positive qualities of the children and the vast amount of innovative and creative work that is taking place in special education.

Labels can affect social and educational expectation and this is particularly relevant to those pupils whose difficulty label receives a double emphasis –

'Profound and Multiple Learning Difficulties' (PMLD). Meeting the needs of the pupils places a positive focus upon the fact that every child can learn. It is easier to plan for new learning when a teacher identifies a need, decides upon a learning route and works together with a child to achieve a goal. The prominence of difficulties makes this process seem impossible – where does a teacher start when she or he receives a description of a child that emphasises the amount of difficulties that the child has? This emphasis upon difficulty does not offer a positive route into the teaching and learning process. In the words of a time-honoured political slogan, 'It's time for change'.

Emotion, behaviour or learning?

Of the three main categories of special school (SLD, MLD and EBD), two place an emphasis on *learning* as a component of difficulty. However, this is not the case for children who are educated in EBD schools. The omission of 'learning' from the title of EBD schools condemns the children to a state of dual dis-location: marginalised from mainstream norms and disenfranchised from the process and product of learning. Their categorisation implies that teachers should focus on pupil feelings, emotions and behavioural difficulties as if these factors are not associated with the learning process. If learning is not em-phasised, what implication does this have for the ideology, pedagogy and curriculum on offer in such schools? Perhaps this dual dislocation might lead us to understand why some EBD schools place an over-emphasis on their therapeutic role, often to the detriment of achievement and attainment through the curriculum. It may also give us an insight into why published statistics from OFSTED (1997) indicate that over 50 per cent of all special schools that are judged to be 'failing' are EBD schools.

How helpful and informative are current labels? Are we meant to assume that the spectrum of children who attend SLD and MLD schools do not have emotional and behavioural difficulties? Do we assume that some children with emotional and behavioural difficulties do not have moderate or severe and profound learning difficulties? Moreover, what should we assume about the emotional and behavioural needs of children whose learning takes place in a 'mainstream', 'regular' or 'ordinary' school?

Children with emotional and behavioural difficulties have a *learning* dif-ficulty – it is an emotional and behavioural learning difficulty. This difficulty highlights an emotional and behavioural learning need. Children with such learning needs are present in all categories of schools and encounter a vast range of curriculum experiences, teaching styles and learning environments. Their challenging behaviour can only change once it is seen as a *learning* difficulty that takes place within the context of the whole child and their whole learning. I have stated that current labels are not helpful when planning teaching; however, I shall use those labels in this book for the purpose of the reader being able to identify the groups of children to whom I am referring. I have also stated that the principles and practices described in this book will apply to all children, but there are particular sections that highlight the needs of those children who present challenging behaviour wherever they are being educated – not contained – educated.

Behaviour and learning

Conceptualising behaviour and learning as separate from each other prevents us from considering the underlying causatory factors that influence a learning difficulty. It is unfortunate, but school policy and teacher practice can reinforce the separation of behaviour and learning. When this happens, and behaviour becomes a challenge, the school confronts it without any clarity about why or how the behaviour relates to the learning process. When we teach children who have learning needs that manifest through their challenging behaviour, we can be drawn into a battle zone if we see behaviour and learning as separate entities. In such a context, a teacher will argue with children and may start to dislike them. It is a sad fact that some teachers at the core of the battle zone will bully children. If behaviour and learning are not seen as interdependent, a teacher can feel personally affronted by a child's behaviour and can allow such behaviour to professionally de-skill them. A school where behaviour and learning are seen as separate may become institutionally manic and employ teaching that is oppressive rather than responsive. Teaching intentions will eventually aim to meet teacher needs rather than those of the pupils.

For the past decade teachers have found themselves travelling at top speed on a white-knuckle ride in the fast lane of national education reform. The lack of consultation between teachers and government caused many to feel that, while the teachers gripped on to their seat belts, the government controlled the steering wheel. This is not to say that all reforms have produced negative outcomes in schools, but the lack of mutual trust will need repairing. At the time when the pace of reform diminished, the *Code of Practice for the Identification and Assessment of Special Educational Needs* (DfE 1994) was introduced.

The Code presented a comprehensive five-stage model of assessment and identification of special educational needs but omitted to apply and extend the model for the purpose of children who attend special schools. Since the inception of the Code of Practice, pupils in special schools rely heavily on the Individual Education Plan (IEP) to receive their curriculum entitlements. The IEP, unfortunately more often about paperwork than pupil work, has also become a tool for the institutionalisation of planning as a process where behaviour and learning can be separated. Some schools are currently writing 'behavioural' IEPs for children whose behaviour is the most prominent feature of their learning need and 'learning' IEPs for children who experience specific cognitive difficulties. If we are aiming to support children in changing their behaviour, it is our professional responsibility to reflect on the complex interplay between the child and the environmental factors that reduce or compound learning difficulties and inhibit or promote new learning. It is time for a national 'wake-up call' for the seamless connection between behaviour and learning to be recognised and evident in schools.

How do you 'see' behaviour?

Once the term 'behaviour' appears in a label associated with a child it usually does not need to be followed by the word 'difficulty'. Used on its own, the assumption will be that we are about to talk of violent, dangerous, anti-social, disruptive or 'naughty' behaviour. It does not imply that we are about to talk of the positive attributes of a child or young person. It also gives no indication that we will be recognising what a child *can* do.

I use the term 'challenging behaviour' in this book because it indicates an approach that demands the consideration of social constructivist principles. There are relevant interacting factors that should be taken into consideration when understanding behaviour and designing intervention. These factors include individual and school pathology, gender, social, economic and cultural factors. Psychological and biological factors must also be considered. The term also indicates that the challenge can be caused by the effect that behaviour has on the lives of others. Overall, it points to the types of behaviour that have a negative and restricting effect on learning development and potential. The term is open to whole-school definition, and thus can also be identified in school policy as behaviour that requires extra support from the school management team.

Zarkowska and Clements (1994) state that between 50 and 60 per cent of children with learning difficulties will present with behaviour difficulties. There is a wealth of literature covering the psychological and sociological perspectives on behaviour (Ayers *et al.* 1995; Cooper *et al.* 1995). Teachers will find this literature a supportive resource in analysing their own perspectives because these have a direct influence on their expectations and responses when teaching children who present challenging behaviour. The teacher should reflect upon the compatibility of their views with the general school view on the location, causation, reduction and extinction of learning difficulties. A teacher must also place their classroom and school in the wider context of other environments in which children learn – accepting that for some children, the out-of-school experience involves a relentless cycle of wall-to-wall deprivation and negativity.

Teacher perceptions

In the everyday, sometimes stressful, practice of working with children who experience learning difficulties and present with challenging behaviour, a teacher's own views of behaviour and learning will determine their style and selection of interventions. I wish to present, in a jargon-free manner, some of the ways in which behaviour is perceived in schools.

- *Behaviour as personal and internal.* There is little hope for children with emotional and behavioural difficulties if teachers view behaviour in this way. From this perspective, the child's behavioural difficulty is located and locked within the child. The child's behaviour and learning potential might even be determined by the surname on their birth certificate. I remember an occasion when I heard a teacher disciplining a pupil outside a classroom. The teacher had reached breaking point and shouted, 'Do you know what the trouble with *you* is?' The teacher was linking the child's behaviour with the child as a person and locating the problem within the child. This is a very personal and potentially confrontational comment to make. The child replied indignantly, 'No I don't (but I'm sure that you are going to tell me).' The teacher was determined to continue with the diagnostic assessment: 'You are just like your . . . .' As I turned the corner I completed this sentence in my head, imagining it to be 'You are just like your brother.' I was wrong. The completed sentence was 'You are just like your father.' The child was then brought back into the classroom. I guessed that it would not be long before he would be out in the corridor again on the receiving end of another high-decibel assessment of causation.

- *Behaviour as external.* This perspective on behaviour claims that a child's challenging behaviour is due to the ineffective systems imposed by the school. The systems are seen to influence and determine a child's behaviour. This view can be used to avoid personal responsibility for the causation of difficulties within a classroom – 'It's the school's fault, not mine.' This perspective can also be presented as a negative explanation for behaviour that is culture-specific.

- *Behaviour as situational and contextual.* This perspective considers behaviour to be influenced by the interaction of critical factors in the environment and in the child. It emphasises that children can experience behaviour difficulties in some settings but may not experience them in others. If a teacher views behaviour in this way the child is likely to be able to make progress in learning. This perspective requires the teacher to reflect on the child and the learning environment and to provide teaching that responds to collective and individual learning styles. It is a perspective which enables the teacher to be a learner too.

- *Behaviour as influenced by medical and organic factors.* This perspective relates behaviour to factors that are part of the child's medical condition and may be described in terms of diagnosis and prognosis. Viewing behaviour in this way also accentuates the relevance of temporary physiological factors such as hunger and tiredness. The teacher aims to understand a child's behaviour through consideration of the child's unique current medical or physiological condition. A medical model does offer a perspective on how a child's need might be altered but it can be unhelpful when quasi-medical causation creeps into phrases such as 'That boy has *got* challenging behaviour.' Where he could have caught it from still baffles me!

- *Behaviour as communication.* It is fundamentally important for teachers to assert the philosophical principle that all children are educable. The logical progression has to be that all children are communicators. From this perspective, all behaviour is seen to be communicating a message. Some of these messages are blatant, for instance when the child threatens you with 'in your face' behaviour: 'Get out of my way or I will throw this chair at you.' Other messages might be just as blatant but more complicated to unravel. A young person with PMLD might fall asleep during a lesson. This may be an unavoidable response to medication, but it might also be an indication of a lack of stimulation. Such behaviour could be saying: 'I'm sixteen, I can't stand the sight of another sticklebrick. I'm bored, offended, and I have had enough.' We have a duty to try to understand the motivational constituents and functional messages of challenging behaviour.

While some teachers will find behaviour difficulties challenging to themselves as professionals, others are challenged in a more personal manner. We have to see a behaviour difficulty within the context of the child as a learner as well as within the wider context of the child as a human being with spiritual, moral, social and cultural needs. The teacher must consider her or his own role in facilitating or frustrating new learning. This process of critical self-reflection enables a teacher to consider what they say and the tone in which they say it, how they teach and the quality of their interactions with children. Teachers have control over the learning environment that they provide. Learning conditions should promote the positive behaviour of the children and the staff.

Meeting individual needs

Behaviour and learning are not separate, and thus we have to be analytical about how we meet the individual learning needs of each child. 'Meeting individual needs' is one of those phrases that permeate our classrooms and our schools. Some teachers will use the term to describe the process of planning, teaching and assessment. It can be used to describe an inclusive approach to meeting a breadth of needs as well as to refer to the development of individualised curriculum programmes. This phrase must be open to conceptual analysis and collaborative discussion. It is incumbent upon schools to define and redefine what 'meeting individual needs' means in the changing context of their own school. Evidence that we are meeting the needs of the individuals must be seen in our planning, teaching and evaluation as well as in our interactions with them.

The phrase 'meeting individual needs' raises many questions for schools. Is it realistic and possible to 'meet' all of the individual needs of each child? When we talk of 'individual' need are we clear about what we mean? Are we not really referring to 'special' needs? Surely all children are special and therefore every teacher in every classroom is continually meeting special educational needs? When we talk of 'needs', isn't this just a politically correct method of referring to difficulties – something that a child cannot do? Are we concerned about describing needs as difficulties because this can be seen as taking a negative standpoint? Isn't difficulty another word for weakness, and doesn't such talk place an emphasis upon those negative aspects that make a child unique? These questions have to be confronted.

Hollow Resonance Syndrome

In aiming or claiming to meet individual needs, we should have evidence that action is taking place in the classroom and throughout the school. If an idea is not put into practice, it can become the victim of 'Hollow Resonance Syndrome' (HRS). In this syndrome, terms, phrases and concepts become part of teacher-talk but not part of teacher-scrutiny. They eventually develop a hollow ring which echoes their lack of real meaning. The hollowness is evident when terms are seen as more useful in public relations exercises than in pupil relations exercises. Teachers who use these terms, and have a commitment to what they mean in practice, can find that accusations fly about how they are jumping on bandwagons or searching for 'buzz words' for their next interview. This is most unfortunate when such terms can encapsulate the essence of an aspect of the art of teaching.

The phrase 'parental partnership' is currently on my HRS 'at-risk' register for this reason. A true test of whether a phrase means something and makes a difference is to talk to those people who are meant to be benefiting from it. Do parents really feel that they have a partnership with the school? What is the power balance in this partnership? Who benefits from the outcomes of the partnership? Does their involvement make any difference at all to the quality of learning in the school? These questions and more should be asked of the pupils when we claim to be meeting their individual needs. What are they learning about their own needs? What are we learning about their needs? Are pupils involved in directing their learning? Do the needs that are being met belong to the pupil or to the teacher? These issues must be addressed.

Needs and difficulties – are they the same and does it matter?

We often talk about 'needs' and 'difficulties' as if they are conceptually the same. They are not. If we are serious about the reunion of learning and behaviour then we have to have conceptual clarity about difficulties and needs and the context in which they occur. I have already stated my preference for a focus upon learning 'needs' rather than learning 'difficulties'. The term 'difficulties' can carry a notion of child deficit and can be stigmatising and discriminatory. It can also be interpreted as a statement of absolutes – these children have difficulties; they will always have difficulties; and teaching wi'l be difficult.

If we are to begin to understand, intervene and change behaviour, we have to analyse our concepts of need and difficulty. This is not a pastime just for the cerebral pleasure of philosophical rumination, although some teachers may enjoy it as such. The reason for being clear about what we mean when we plan to teach is to enable us to be better at what we do when we are teaching. Understanding how we construct definitions of 'need' and 'difficulty' can ensure that there is a direct link between our teaching and learning intentions.

Figure 1.1 shows the conceptual interrelationship between need, provision, and difficulty. The process of learning requires the movement from one learning position to a new position. In Figure 1.1, this journey is illustrated as the progress from point A to point B. For children who experience learning difficulties, this journey is not a straightforward one. There is a conceptual gap between A and B which has to be negotiated and it is here that the child's difficulty lies. The learning difficulty is composed of the combination of any number of interactive factors between the child and the environment. Sometimes a child's response to difficulty is to seek to obscure it. We talk of a child 'digging a hole' when they seem to encounter a difficulty. This hole may

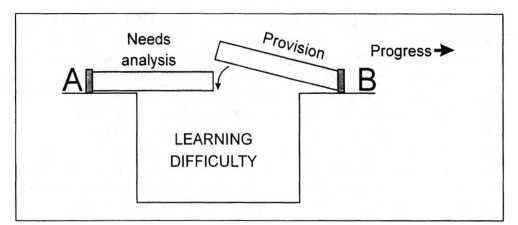

Figure 1.1   Bridging the learning difficulty gap

be an initial hiding place or it might be a place where the child flounders in a state of increasing anxiety. It becomes deeper and more difficult to escape from unless the teacher identifies the provision that will bridge the learning difficulty gap. Relevant provision will prevent the child from becoming further entrenched in their difficulty. When determining provision, the teacher must consider how the learning difficulty can change in relation to the context and perspective in which it occurs.

Theory into practice

The importance of a theoretical conceptualisation of need and difficulty becomes evident when it is applied to the daily work of a teacher. An eight-year-old girl who presents challenging behaviour starts a new term, in a new class, in an MLD school. The school already has concerns about the increasing complexity of its recent intake of children. The new girl has limited communication and interactive skills and can be physically violent towards pupils and adults. Staff room rumours abound about how difficult she is and some staff are claiming that this girl should be in an SLD school. They articulate a definition of her learning difficulties – 'She's too SLD for us.' Her previous teacher has said that her new teacher will have to control the girl's behaviour before the child will even start to learn. The new teacher wishes to promote positive behaviour but the girl has acquired such a negative reputation that it seems impossible to establish any positive aspects of her behaviour.

Here are two possible scenarios that might appear at the extremes of a continuum. Both involve choices that are blunt, real, and will affect the pupil's quality of life. The teacher can concentrate on the child's difficulties thereby confusing them with her needs. If her initial focal point is one of difficulties, she will become overwhelmed by problems, separate the girl's behaviour from her learning and may ultimately develop practice where teacher need dominates pupil need. The focus on insuperable difficulties, particularly when they affect the learning potential of other pupils, can cause the child and the teacher to join each other in the difficulty gap and to develop negative relationship patterns. In the murky depths of the difficulty gap, alternative approaches are not visible and the opportunities for the mutual development of new skills are buried. In this situation, the child and teacher dig a deeper hole together – the difficulty gap now becomes a difficulty chasm. It will not be long before the teacher joins the staff room campaign for the child to change schools.

This emphasis on difficulties can now become applied as a tool for the metamorphosis of the school admissions policy. A document that originally indicated the needs that the school curriculum can meet becomes one for identifying difficulties that the school will reject. The admissions policy, in defiance of its title, becomes a charter for keeping children out rather than one for allowing them in.

The second scenario involves identifying the need and prescribing the provision required to bridge the learning difficulty gap. The teacher can select a priority goal so that the child can move from A to B. The teacher will pay attention to the detail of the learning environment and how the child's need determines their interaction with it. A flexible and responsive pedagogical attitude will support a child in overcoming difficulties in a classroom where the child feels welcome and valued. The final decision may be that the child should attend an SLD school. However, the professional judgement is based on the match between the child's needs and the curriculum, resources and teaching styles required to meet those needs. The teacher and the school must be responsive to learning needs rather than reactive to learning difficulties.

My assertion is that there is a critical interactive relationship between need and difficulty but they are not the same. This distinction enables us to have a more optimistic and positive outlook in relation to developing respectful environments that can alter learning difficulties and meet learning needs. If a child is to develop a positive and responsive relationship with the teacher, their needs should never be saturated and submerged by their difficulties. If the child needs a respectful relationship, the teacher must enter it accepting that there will be learning difficulties. The message for the child is ' I know that you may hit or kick me but I am aware that you need to develop a positive relationship with someone. I am that person. I will show you that we can begin to change those difficulties and it is possible for someone to enjoy being with you.'

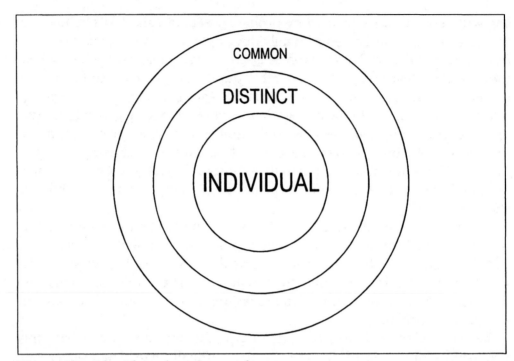

Figure 1.2   Identifying learning needs

Needs and difficulties are not the same and understanding the difference does matter because it affects a teacher's ability to teach and a child's ability to learn.

Which needs are we meeting?

Working in special education, it is easy for differences to become the starting point for identifying learning need. However, if we are to value every single child as part of the learning community, it is important that we first recognise the commonalities between children. All children have needs that are related to their personhood, their development within a group, and their individual characteristics. Figure 1.2 identifies these learning needs as 'common, distinct and individual'.

Common needs

The starting point for need identification begins with recognising those needs that are common to all children. These needs identify a child as a member of the human race. Common needs will include, among others, a need to feel a sense of belonging, a need to communicate and to be communicated with, and a need to be respected. Every child, no matter how challenging their behaviour might be or how profound their learning difficulty appears, should be afforded the dignity of interactions that respect them as humans and learners. This will allow them to develop a positive understanding of their relationship with the world around them and help them to take a step along the pathway towards a sense of holistic spiritual, moral and cultural well being.

Distinct needs

The process of need identification continues by recognising those distinct needs that belong to groups of children. In the broader context, we have to identify needs that relate to those groups to which children belong; for example, there will be needs that females have that males do not have and vice versa. In the educational context, distinct needs can refer to large groupings such as those children who experience severe learning difficulties, emotional and behavioural difficulties, or those who attend mainstream schools. It may also relate to the distinct needs of smaller groups that are continually re-constructed in the school environment. Cultural and faith communities to which children belong highlight distinct needs that should be recognised in the classroom.

Individual needs

Once distinct needs have been identified, the teacher is in a position to establish the individual needs of a particular child at a particular time in a particular context. It is important to emphasise that once the individual need has been established it is not made invisible if the child is working as a member of a group – it is not subsumed by distinct needs. Clarity about what constitutes an individual need enables a school to become analytical about its provision. This will involve critical and sometimes harsh self-reflection.

A school may discover that the content of its IEPs prevents them from meeting individual needs. The IEP content may describe targets that remain in the area of distinct learning needs. A 'distinct' education plan will never be applicable to the education of a particular individual. The situation is more serious if the content of the plan renders it a 'common' education plan. If IEPs are to be meaningful components of the teaching and learning process they have to address *individual* needs and involve those individuals that they claim to support. This brings sense and meaning to a process that is in danger of becoming a pointless practice that builds a paper mountain and gets in the way of teaching. A child should be a participant in their IEP not a victim of it.

Needs and provision

Educational needs will be met within various dimensions and structures of provision (Fish 1989; Fish and Evans 1995) and may require the support of Health and Social Services. Effective communication is imperative when a variety of agencies and individuals become stakeholders in the setting of the long- and short-term goals for the education of an individual child. Inter-service liaison can help to illuminate the reasons why particular needs may be prioritised in different ways by different services. In ensuring that the need is not confused with the difficulty, the teacher should also pay close attention to the difference between the need and the provision required to meet the need.

Table 1.1 illustrates the starting point for provision that will meet the three types of need.

Table 1.1 Needs and provision

Need	Meeting place (provision)
Common needs Needs which are common to all humans	**The educational context** The broad aims of education – e.g. self determination, social interaction, achievement of potential, rights to access, spiritual and moral development . . .
Distinct needs Needs associated with being a member of a group or community	**The educational setting** School category – mainstream school or special school
Individual needs Needs relating to a particular pupil at a particular time	**The school setting** *This* mainstream school or *this* special school (EBD, MLD, SLD . . .)

The term 'special need' does not appear on Table 1.1 nor does it appear in Figure 1.2. Although this term asserts the right of a child to receive particular educational provision, it may not help a teacher gain clarity about the need that they are meeting. This confusion may reduce the quality of teaching. In the education system, the word 'special' is used in a multiplicity of contexts often without clarity of reference to the need or combination of needs that it is referring to. Some colleagues adopt the term 'special' to describe a need that is individual or unique – 'every child is special to me'. I have heard this definition of 'special' being used as a reason why a special needs policy is not necessary in a special school – 'Why should we have a special needs policy?

After all, every child in the school has special needs'. Here, the manipulation of the term 'special' lacks contextual integrity.

The term 'special need' can be used to describe needs that are distinct within a certain group – for example, a physically disabled child may have some needs that are particular to a group of similarly disabled children and others that he would share with a wider group such as the disabled community. He will also have needs that are common to all children and needs that are individual and unique. This child may also find that others use the term 'special' as a label that attracts stigmatisation and discrimination or sympathy and charity. Norwich (1996) uses the word 'exceptional' to avoid this type of conceptual confusion as well as highlighting the positive connotations of such a term.

The legal statement of 'special' educational need does not always help the teacher to plan the provision that is required to meet the need because it might never pinpoint a child's individual needs. In some cases a statement will indicate that a child requires a broad and balanced curriculum, with clear achievable steps, supported by regular links with parents, and positive encouragement by staff. This is a statement of common learning need. Other criteria set out in a statement may go no further than describing need that is distinct to defined categories of children who have special educational needs. It is only when specific individual needs are identified that it can and will become a central tool for planning a curriculum that will meet the holistic needs of the pupil.

The case of two hypothetical children who have cerebral palsy, which is identified as a special educational need, can illustrate my point about the term 'special'. Their special educational need, which identifies them as part of a group, highlights their distinct needs in terms of school placement and statutory provision. The decision about provision must be based on their individual needs not solely on their distinct needs – it cannot be assumed that all children with cerebral palsy have the same individual needs, nor can judgements be made without a comprehensive knowledge of the child as an individual. Though these two pupils have the same disability, they will have different individual needs. This might result in one being educated in mainstream provision while the other requires the specialist provision and approach of a particular special school. A similar situation and outcome may apply to two children experiencing emotional and behavioural difficulties. Clearly, their distinct needs may be the same but their individual needs could be completely different.

My assertion is that the progressive focusing upon need must begin with 'common' and end with 'individual'. The term 'special' has come, through over- and misuse, to cloud conceptual clarity and prevent precision in planning for new learning. The multi-purpose use of the term 'special' can turn the systematic process of planning needs-driven teaching into an unfocused and interminable journey through a maze of disconnected and meaningless learning experiences. If we intend to value children as individuals, we must accept that two children can have the same special educational need but that a child's individual need, in any context or at any given time, is by definition unique.

What can I do in the classroom?

When planning to meet a need, a teacher has to undertake a process of need analysis and assessment that must inform the planning of teaching and learning. Figure 1.3 illustrates a model for such a process, and its rigorous application enables it to be relevant to the full range of learning needs. At each stage of the process, the teacher is confronted by a main question that will be answered by considering other subsidiary questions.

Five analytical questions

The 'state' question – What is the current learning state for the child?
It is necessary to make an assessment of the current learning situation and establish a baseline. In doing so, consideration should be given to the strengths and needs that the child and the environment bring to this current learning state. Previous assessment will support the answer to the 'state' question. A teacher's concept of need will influence the baseline that they wish to establish and there should be clarity about the need or needs that a teacher aims to meet. The establishment of a baseline is not a need analysis in itself – it is the starting point.

The 'goal' question – What do I want the child to achieve?
The next stage in the process is to decide what the main learning goal for the child will be. The goal that is chosen must be related to the child's need. Teachers should explore the likes and interests of the pupil when setting a goal. It should be described in a positive manner – for example, ' When this goal is achieved, the pupil *will* . . . .' The goal must make demands upon the child but also remain realistic. There has to be a clear distinction between what the teacher is teaching and the learning need of the child. This ensures that the teacher is clear about the difference between the goal and the child's need. It is important that the goal should not be confused with a broad aim – aims do not provide the specific focus for a curriculum activity. The setting of goals for any child does not take place in isolation and is influenced by the political, cultural and social context of the curriculum. Our own values and assumptions about learning theory will also influence it.

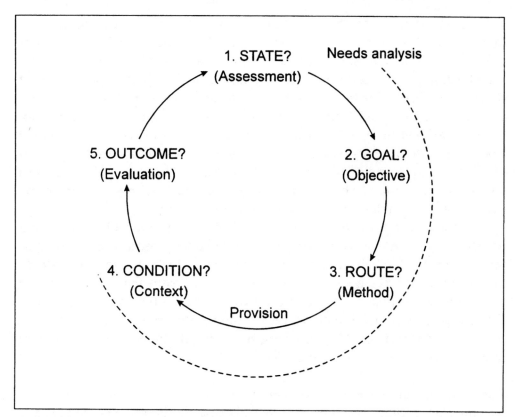

Figure 1.3   Five analytical questions

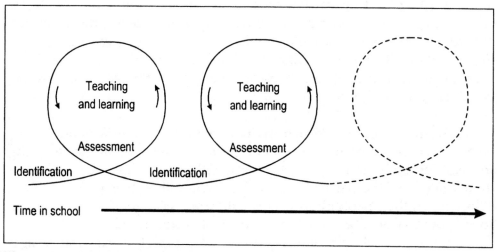

Figure 1.4   The learning cycle

The goal should be practicable, achievable and have meaning and relevance for the child. When setting a goal a teacher must consider how they will assess if the child has achieved it. Success criteria must be explicit – what will the child be doing when they have achieved the goal and with what percentage of success? A teacher has to decide if every task they set requires 100 per cent accuracy when assessed. Children who experience learning difficulties may not be able to achieve or repeat total and complete accuracy in every task that they attempt and should not be subjected to the tedium, frustration or denigration of being forced to do so. This means that the teacher must recognise the times when task performance becomes nothing more than hoop jumping for the sake of it and is unrelated to new and extended learning.

I choose to use the word 'goal' instead of 'learning target' or 'learning objective' although all three are interchangeable. I do this because 'goal' conjures up an image of a football game and gives me a visual metaphor to work with. In the classroom, focused goal setting for children will ensure that they can score a goal as quickly as possible. Of course, the overall aim will help them to do this. The goalposts will need to be nearer to some children than to others and a positive teacher will continue offering support until the last minute of extra time so that every child can be successful.

The 'route' question – How do *we* get there?
An emphasis is placed on the word 'we' because a child must be involved. If autonomy and independence are meaningful aims for a school community, the child should be a contributor to the process of teaching. Need analysis and learning progression will be most productive when teaching is seen as a communicative and interactive process. If possible, the child should be involved in providing information that will help to describe and determine the desired learning route. The child should be able to identify what the goal is and what they will be doing, thinking or saying when they have achieved it.

There is an umbilical link between the 'route' for learning and the 'condition' in which it occurs.

The 'condition' question – Which environment is the most effective?
When considering how to meet a child's needs, we must examine the teaching and learning environment. A teacher has to reflect upon how they can meet a child's needs in the particular school in which they teach. This will be influenced by the school culture of curriculum and pedagogy and involves an honest appraisal of the potential environment that is required.

It is at this point that the interrelationship between the need and what is required to meet the need – 'provision' – becomes evident. As Table 1.1 indicates there has to be a separation between the need and the place in which the need is met. This allows teachers to remain focused and analytical about the driving force behind decisions that are made about, and on behalf of, children who experience learning difficulties. On a macro level, a teacher can determine whether need or provision is the main factor in educational placement. On a micro level, they can become more effective in designing individual learning experiences. When considering the learning route and the learning condition the interplay between the dimensions of need and provision provokes two important subsidiary questions:

(a) What provision is ideally available?
(b) What provision is really available?

To answer in the best interest of children, provision should be seen in its broadest sense, which includes material and human resources. Human resources are not only composed of teachers and learning assistants, they also include parents and the professional support network. The skills and competencies of those who work within and for services that are dedicated to the improvement of learning are an influential factor in the potential success of such provision. Effective deployment of provision necessitates a professional response that does not shy away from defining and evaluating the responsibilities and roles of the provision task force.

Colleagues will recognise a situation where a Local Education Authority (LEA) might provide extra support hours for a child who has learning difficulties. They will also be aware that this will make no quantifiable difference at all unless roles and responsibilities are clear. Increased time allocation for learning support does not miraculously produce improved quality of learning. The crucial aspects of provision, such as the curriculum programmes that are tailored to the child's needs and the contexts in which they can be made available, must be evaluated at regular intervals. When applying this model, an outcome of an analysis might be that special school provision is no longer essential and mainstream schooling is now required. It would be conceptually acceptable to state that the child *needs* a different school.

The reality of teaching is that, while we are able to describe the 'ideally' available provision, we are forced to prescribe the 'really' available provision. A teacher can be constrained by the resources at their disposal inside and outside their school but the responsibility to do their best for the child with the available provision still remains. It is amazing the way in which so many teachers use their energy and creativity to work wonders with limited stimulus materials. Teachers have to advocate for improved provision but cannot postpone teaching until all imaginable resources are in place.

The 'outcome' question – Have we arrived at the new learning state?
We can only judge if a need has been met by gaining evidence of whether the child has travelled from an initial baseline to a new desired learning state. This assessment and evaluation process should involve the child in assessing and recognising their own progress and should not limit the collection of evidence to written outcomes.

The cyclical nature of this model provides the licence for the teacher and the child to return to the start of the process, establish a new baseline, and identify a new need. The focus on *learning* is absolutely vital. Throughout this process a teacher will consider what a child is learning in conjunction with what a child is doing. The distinction between 'doing' and 'learning' ensures that teachers can avoid the trap of reporting on curriculum coverage (what a child has done) instead of reporting on curriculum outcomes (what a child has learnt).

Figure 1.4 shows how this model is incorporated into an ongoing process.

There are similarities between how the model operates and the Hindu concept of reincarnation. It is a Hindu belief that the soul takes on a body until the body ceases to exist, at which point the soul is reborn into a new body. The cycle of birth and rebirth takes place over time. In Figure 1.4, a need is identified and teaching takes place until the need ceases to exist. A new need is identified and teaching takes place until that particular need is met. The cyclical model of need identification takes place over a time sequence that is relative to the individual child. In the concept of the transmigration of the soul, good actions will result in rewards so that the soul is in a more favourable position for improved quality of life. This model aims to demonstrate that good teaching offers beneficial rewards so that the child is in a more favourable position for improved quality of life.

Teaching reality or virtual reality?

Let us consider the application of this model to the case of a five year old girl called Smarika, who has a great sense of fun and loves to draw. Her language delay does cause her frustrations and can be a factor in producing challenging behaviour. When she arrives in the morning, her teacher is able to make an instant assessment of the type of day that might be in store. Smarika's body language and the speed of her entrance into the room are two indicators. When Smarika is unhappy, she will storm to her desk and will not talk to anybody. Even the use of her name, or a subtle attempt to engage her in a task, can result in self-injurious face slapping and hurling of equipment. Evidently, her need includes being able to communicate to staff about how she feels and to understand that there are acceptable ways for her to do so. Her teacher knows that Smarika can understand the symbolic representation of happiness and sadness because she enjoys smiley faces for her good work and identifies sad characters by their mouths when they read stories together.

Applying the model

Smarika and her teacher cut two large circles out of card and Smarika draws a happy face on one and a sad face on the other. Before progressing further, her teacher checks that Smarika can identify which of these faces is happy and which sad – she can. The teacher discusses Smarika's goal with her and explains that when she enters the classroom in the morning she has permission to collect one of these faces and attach it to a chart by her desk. Smarika will select the face that represents how she is feeling and inform the adults through this method. When she does so, an adult will make immediate recognition of the chosen face and offer Smarika space to settle in the classroom. The teacher will design a meaningful reward for her and she will receive it for informing adults of her current mood. The reward may be instant or cumulative. The teacher can remind Smarika of the plan for the morning – perhaps through the use of photographs or symbols (Detheridge and Detheridge 1997). There will be an expectation that she has to do her work and a time limit for starting the work might be set by using a sand timer or a clock as a visual cue.

The teacher will design a method for reducing the use of the faces and will have to decide how frequently they should be used before a new method is required. Some element of reducing the prompt is necessary and the teacher should give Smarika increasing control over the use of this intervention. The teacher may decide upon 100 per cent usage in the first two weeks and allow reduced usage after that. It is not the type of strategy that the teacher would use for a long period of time because once Smarika has 'got it', expectation of future developments and success must be raised.

In this learning process, the teacher has moved Smarika from position A to position B based on what is a 'really' available route in his classroom. Smarika will learn about the purpose, context and effectiveness of communication. At the outcome stage, the teacher will have documented evidence that this intervention is working and may wish to introduce a future goal. This might involve Smarika indicating her feelings, visually or orally, with a more complex range of feelings to discriminate from. The teacher might introduce tired, hungry, and angry, to give both of them an insight into the feelings that are creating the challenging behaviour. However, it may be that the teacher sets a completely different priority goal relating to literacy.

The model applies to the process and the product of *learning* and therefore it will work just as well for the reduction of Smarika's challenging behaviour as it will for the improvement of her literacy skills. When there is conceptual clarity about the nature of individual learning needs and how they can be met, teachers can provide an environment that promotes positive behaviour rather than producing challenging behaviour.

The whistling dog

I am unable to name the source of this story, although since I have adopted the urban folk tradition of embellishing it for my own purpose, it now bears little resemblance to its original composition.

It concerns a man who is a regular at a local pub, but has not been there for three months. His friends have missed him and are delighted when he returns one evening carrying his dog underneath his arm. For the ethical purpose of ensuring canine anonymity, I shall call the dog 'Muffin'. One of his friends rushes over and she asks, 'Where have you been for the past three months?' He explains, 'I have spent the last three months teaching my dog how to whistle.' His friends laugh, thinking that he is joking.

They decide that an immediate assessment is required and one of them challenges him to provide some evidence, 'I don't believe you – let's hear your dog whistle'. The owner agrees and places his dog on the floor. Muffin is asked to whistle but does not respond. One of the owner's friends decides to kneel down to be at the same physical level as the dog, and making supportive eye contact, repeats his instruction in an encouraging tone,

'C'mon Muffin, whistle, good boy, c'mon.' The dog stares at him, growling quietly, and looking particularly confused. The man is undeterred by this and begins to model the behaviour that he requires. Intermittently whistling, he prompts the dog again 'Whistle . . . c'mon Muffin . . . whistle.' The dog's growling develops into a mild snarl, but there is still no discernible evidence of whistling. After a few more attempts, the man raises his voice and begins to click his fingers next to the dog's mouth, as if irritated by the whole experience – 'C'mon dog, you are supposed to be able to whistle, let's hear you whistle – now.' At this point Muffin moves his head, opens his mouth, and takes a large bite out of the man's hand. Leaping up in pain, the man shrieks out to the owner 'I thought you said you had spent the last three months teaching your dog how to whistle?' 'I have,' replied the owner 'but I did not say that he had learnt how to do it!'

The messages about teaching and learning are obvious. The messages about teacher and learner behaviour are painfully obvious.

Chapter 2

The management of teaching and learning

I would like to consider many of the issues that surround the management of teaching and learning for children who find learning a challenge. My main emphasis will be on children with learning difficulties and associated emotional and behavioural difficulties. The principles will apply to all special and mainstream schools but I shall begin by considering the important points to be made about schools that cater specifically for children who have emotional and behavioural difficulties, the group of children whose perceived failure has resulted in new government initiatives for early identification and intervention (DfEE 1997).

Emotional and behavioural difficulties

There are moments of great fun and pleasure teaching children who ex-perience emotional and behavioural difficulties. There are also moments when the demands of the pupils can empty your personal resources, challenge your self-belief, and create a huge 'give and take' imbalance in the mutually responsive relationships that we aim to develop with children. Working with children who find it difficult to be helped, in an environment where some are ashamed to attend, is a challenge to any professional. Pupils in a special school may identify the learning benefits of attending the school, but share in a devalued identity due to the stigmatising perceptions of mainstream peers (Norwich 1997).

When you make a commitment to teach children in an EBD school you learn a great deal about yourself as a professional and as a person. Emotional strength and professional integrity are required when you provide a wide range of teaching and learning intentions and an individual, or the whole class, does their best to hijack your teaching. Finely tuned observational skills are necessary when a teacher encounters the emotional and physical language of the classroom. This requires a sensitive awareness of the meaning of verbal and non-verbal language and a conscious knowledge of the impact of each interaction that a teacher makes with individuals and groups.

While children with emotional and behavioural difficulties exist in various schools, it is in the EBD school that they are gathered together displaying their sophisticated skills of curriculum dodging and task evasion that are often associated with a low self-image. I have been critical of the assumptions associated with many of the labels that permeate the world of special needs education. In relation to the management of teaching and learning I wish to emphasise the relevance and importance of one particular label – 'School'.

By definition, a teacher working in a school has a professional responsibility to provide learning opportunities for every pupil. The 'work models' and ideologies of teachers and schools must be examined so that a school can develop and advance. Teachers should be encouraged to reflect upon their own ideology and work model.

Work models – teacher and school compatibility

Teachers bring their own work model to their place of work. This model may be influenced by their own experience of schooling and will include a pedagogical approach based upon opinions and beliefs about how children learn. A teacher functions within an organisational model that implements the school's aims and ethos. This model can only be implemented when teachers are skilled in critical reflection because, without such skills, schools can become static and unresponsive institutions. A responsive school will make the distinction between management, which may make it stagnant, and leadership, which will offer vision and development.

The pedagogical attitude of the teacher can be a causal factor in the elimination or provocation of emotional and behavioural difficulties. The Code of Practice (DfE 1994) states:

> Emotional and behavioural difficulties may result, for example, from abuse or neglect; physical or mental illness; sensory or physical impairment or psychological trauma. In some cases, emotional and behavioural difficulties may arise from or be exacerbated by circumstances within the school environment. (para. 3:65)

The school should be clear about the ideologies that it decides to adopt and a teacher should aim to find a school that offers compatibility with their own work model. When this is the case, the teacher will promote good practice and should have the courage to openly reject bad practice. If a teacher is aware of another colleague's disrespectful behaviour towards a pupil, then the teacher should not comply with it; it should be confronted and challenged. This principle applies to any school where an undignified or aversive intervention is used.

Teacher work model

A fundamental issue in the teacher's work model is commitment. If a teacher chooses to work with children with a wide range of learning difficulties, they make a commitment to a certain style of working. In an EBD school, a teacher will provide new learning for a range of children – some of whom may have severe psychiatric illness. Some may be coming to terms with abuse, and others may have found it difficult to cope with the pace of mainstream curriculum progression. Their learning needs may be long-, short- or medium-term. In such a setting the teacher must be self-confident, flexible and have developed a range of strategies for preventing and dealing with stressful and distressing challenging situations. The skill of thinking on your feet is vital, and a sense of humour is a primary requirement.

Children who have a low self-image need to see that the adults working in their school enjoy being there. In such an environment, the adults work collaboratively and offer collegial support; they model friendly and respectful behaviour; they say that they like to teach the children and they demonstrate that they are proud of where they work. After all, they have made a choice to work there; nobody has dragged them in off the streets under duress. The adults should transmit a feeling that the school is a good place to be. Most importantly and whenever possible they laugh with each other, with the children, but never at them.

Without this enjoyment the EBD school can become a demoralised and depressing institution where low morale is exported with depressing rapidity. The teacher should be an exponent of responsive pedagogy (Daniels 1996) and the school management should develop a responsive school culture where pupil and teachers are motivated and where all learners have a voice. The work model of a teacher in an EBD school must contain a willingness to offer a fresh start to each child every day. Teachers must give themselves, or be given, a fresh start too – approaching each day with optimism and a commitment to improving the quality of learning in the school. Without this willingness the teacher will enter the desperate state of mind where they feel that there are only three bad days in an EBD school – yesterday, today and tomorrow.

Effective school or ineffective youth club?

There are many current tensions about the issue of how learning in schools for children with emotional and behavioural difficulties should be managed (Peagam 1995). Ideological standpoints and institutional management can produce a range and variety of EBD provision. We have to be aware of pupils' perceptions of their school and the loyalty that pupils would like to have to where they are taught. There is no reason why an EBD school should not promote loyalty and pride among the pupils, offer high expectation and demand high standards. EBD schools should aim to demonstrate the features of an effective school (Ainscow 1991; Sammons *et al.* 1996).

Matthew is a Year 10 pupil who attended an all-age EBD school that was placed under 'special measures'. He joined the school when he was seven and resents having been there for so long. The school began to change when he was eleven, and he perceived a new ideology and a new emphasis. He describes the change in the learning environment:

> The school looked like a playing centre – a youth club but an old and dirty one. There were settees in the classroom; graffiti, swearing all the time . . . and you could play pool if you didn't want to work. Just argue with the teacher and then you play pool instead of that lesson – easy. Think about it! Then it started to change, and it was all different. It looked clean, and there was children's work on the walls, and we started to do school things like having assembly and teachers telling us what the lessons were about – but using our words to explain. It even looks like a real school now except little children are in the same school as big children.

Matthew is an example of a pupil who believed in the maxim, 'I am rubbish, my school is rubbish and therefore my teachers must be the most rubbish ones available.' He would have articulated this feeling in less polite terms. While it is part of a teacher's role to change Matthew's self-concept, his school-concept needs changing too. Clarity about the function of the school is imperative.

What type of school do we want to be?

The whole school community can operate as a supportive task force in implementing an ethos that values the common, distinct and individual needs of pupils with emotional and behavioural difficulties. As with school inspection, school concept and ethos is not something which teachers should stand by and allow to happen to them. We have control over how our schools develop, and we must have high expectations of what the children can achieve. Social, economic, emotional or cognitive disadvantage should not be compounded by low expectation of progress and success.

A learning organisation should review and reflect upon its ability to produce high standards in teaching and learning and particular schools should ask particular questions. Here are *some* of the questions an EBD school should use to challenge itself – although some are EBD-specific, many are relevant to all schools.

- *Are we providing distinct and specialist provision?* Expectation must be high, but there must also be a realistic understanding of how emotional and behavioural difficulties can affect the pace of learning within the school. A special school is a form of distinct provision and provides for a distinct community. The special school is not a mini-mainstream school – the children are there for a reason. An EBD school has to reflect the needs of its pupils, and it will do this through its curricular provision. It will pay particular attention to pace of learning and the distinct element of its non-National Curriculum time. Some children will have lost faith in mainstream school and will rightly expect that the existence of a high level of staff–pupil ratio will meet their learning needs and offer them something different. Pupils have an entitlement to expect something 'special' from a special school.

- *Are our goals focused on the educational needs of our pupils?* In an EBD school, the children should receive the National Curriculum. The remaining curriculum time might be focused on their distinct and particular social and emotional needs. There may be a higher input of personal and social education, for example, through the use of 'circle time' (Goldthorpe 1998). This would require the introduction of structured, planned sessions aimed at improving the skills of talking, listening and problem solving through a circle time model (Moseley 1997). Educational goals must be the focus of a school. An EBD school should promote educational attainment not social containment.

- *Are our goals focused on the educational difficulties of our pupils?* The emphasis on difficulty places a contingent emphasis on overcoming the difficulty. This can result in difficulties being perceived as impairments and thus the school may decide, or suddenly discover, that a whole-school therapeutic approach is being adopted.

- *Are we aware of the topography of needs within the school and do we have a view on their alterability?* The school will make judgements about the long- and short-term needs of the children. The judgements about how changeable learning needs will be should be based on the environment that the school provides and the interaction between the pupil and that environment. A school should not reject the influence that external models and systems can have on altering need.

- *Do our policies make a difference?* There should be a clear relationship between school policies and the nature of the children in the school. The policies should describe philosophical rationale and its practical application. They should give guidance to staff. The principles of a policy should be reviewed as regularly as the procedures in order to maintain whole-school consistency and relevance.

- *Are parents a part of the school or apart from it?* Parental involvement in special schools may take special efforts. Most children travel by LEA transport and most parents are not to be seen bringing their children to school or collecting them at the end of the day. Parents can feel guilty about their child's placement in a special school, and while remaining sensitive to this, the school must give proof to the parents that the placement is a positive step.

   Relationships with parents should be reciprocal (Mittler and Mittler 1994). When schools design successful interventions that reduce challenging behaviour, they must share their expertise with parents. This must be done in a non-patronising way that does not make value judgements about parental blame. Similarly, parents can share their strategies with the school. Parents should be contacted when things are going well, not only at times of crisis. The opportunity to understand and become informed about parental rights should apply to all parents not just to those who are articulate and perceived as middle-class. Parents will feel part of the school when it supports them in asserting their rights.

- *Are we using our support services in the best interests of the children?* Effective liaison between the school and the LEA, the therapy services, the psychological service, health and social services must be a priority. However liaison itself is not good enough. The school should consider the active role of these services in meeting the individual needs of pupils. The educational psychologist is not just a resource for writing statutory reports and attending Annual Review meetings. Creative planning can ensure that the school's attached educational psychologist becomes a rich resource for curriculum development and improving teachers' knowledge of the learning process. The Annual Review meeting is one area in which curriculum development should take place. The school should maximise and prioritise psychologist time so that she or he is involved in the process of differentiation. The psychologist should be seen in class, released from the mind-numbing rigours of commercially produced observation schedules, responding to the emerging needs of children as an active member of the school's differentiation task force. I know from experience that it can be done successfully.

- *Is reintegration into mainstream an aspiration for all?* EBD schools do themselves and the pupils a great disservice by presenting return to mainstream school as the optimal and utopian outcome for all pupils. The aim of a return to mainstream for all might not take individual needs into account – it also provides a negative image of the school. The hidden message that pupils may receive is that their school must be a bad school because the greatest success is to escape from it. What does this say to pupils about the quality of education provided in the school? The isolating aspect of special schools can be a damaging outcome of a placement, but a programme of whole-class integration links with a mainstream school can provide a wider peer group. Individual integration arrangements according to individual need may result in some children receiving a successful full-time mainstream placement relevant to their needs.

- *Are we the last resort for our pupils?* There is an immense danger in presenting the school in this manner. Pupils may feel rejected and punished by being 'sent' to an EBD school and to present the school as a last resort reinforces that rejection and punishment. It becomes a place where children make active decisions not to engage in what the school offers. Let's be honest, who can blame them if the negative outcomes seem to outweigh the positive ones?

- *Are we the last resort for our staff?* The school development plan must offer a financially costed commitment to staff training. A staff room culture of berating people who are on courses, by claiming that those who are left behind are the ones that really care about the children, is one that must be counteracted.

  In fact the term 'left behind' adequately describes what can happen to those staff who are do not attend courses to update their knowledge and develop their skills. The belief that training to be a teacher stops once you actually become a teacher must be challenged. As Carpenter (1996) reminds us, children are now entering our schools 'the like of whom we have never seen before.' This places demands upon teachers to develop new skills that will provide learning for children who present us with increasingly complex and unpredictable learning styles. To teach well, a teacher has to continue to learn and some of the learning opportunities are provided in situations that are external to the school.

Setting whole school aims

School aims should direct and justify the curriculum offered and the pedagogy that is employed. The aims should be encapsulated in the interactions between all members of the school community. I would like to refer to the process of aim-setting at Alexandra School in South Harrow as it was one of the methods employed to turn a failing environment into a flourishing one. I am not presenting the school as an exemplar of good practice, but describing the process for colleagues who are currently in a similar position. The dangers of arrogant and sanctimonious complacency should be guarded against, because it is a short distance for a halo to travel before it becomes a noose.

The school initially had four stated aims all couched in language that was difficult to interpret and assess in practice. In fact, the four aims were combined to create a rather long mission statement. In the restating of school aims at Alexandra, a mission statement was avoided – mission statements are also on my HRS 'at-risk' register! Aims were specific and implementation indicators were established. This ensures that the aims were taking place in practice and could be open to redefinition because of practice.

Alexandra School aims

The school community gathered together for a training day. The community included all of the people who had regular involvement with the children including the school meals supervisor and the school secretary. It also included representatives from external support services whom we saw as crucial in the implementation of a new shared vision for the school. Many members of the Governing Body attended. All voices had to be heard, as it was not justifiable to have any person there on bogus grounds. The outcome of the day was the compilation of a set of comprehensive aims that described how the school would function in five main areas.

At this early stage of institutional change we were developing an emerging clarity about the types and levels of learning need that we were aiming to meet. We identified how our pupils might develop within an early design of the concentric notion of three types of learning need (see Figure 1.2). We were also aiming to set explicit goals for school development. The following constitutes a selection from each of the five areas:

1. *The school and the curriculum.* To provide a broad and balanced curriculum which includes the National Curriculum. To promote moral, spiritual, cultural and physical development. To engage and motivate learners in a curriculum which reflects individual diversity. To meet the

learning needs that are common to all children, common to children who attend special schools, and those needs that are particular to an individual child at a particular time.

2. *The school as an environment for learning.* To establish an ethos where children share our positive regard for the school as a learning environment. To ensure that the building is as attractive as possible because this demonstrates that we value the children, the learning process and our own work.

3. *The school and the whole individual.* To remember that the children and young people bring complex social and emotional needs to school, and that these needs must be addressed. To involve pupils in the planning, assessment and evaluation of their own work.

4. *The school and the community.* To work hard to maintain good communication with and support from our parents and carers. To develop a positive image of the school as an important part of the community.

5. *The school as an institution which provides professional development and support.* To improve our ability as a school and as individuals to teach and support children with a broad range of learning needs through a commitment to in-service training and professional development. To communicate effectively and consult widely so that the decision making process is understood and decisions are made and implemented.

(from Alexandra School Aims 1994)

The specificity of these aims enabled the school to implement a corporate model of school development planning (MacGilchrist *et al.* 1995) where priority aims were selected each year and assessed in terms of financial, human and time resources. The school's new emphasis on learning and curriculum is enshrined in these aims and supported the process of continually reminding the pupils that they were in a *school* and therefore they were there to learn. The aims were also open to evaluation and restatement and were not complacently carved in the school's tablets of eternity.

Curriculum or therapy?

There is a tension between the competing ideologies that exist in the field of educating children who experience emotional and behavioural difficulties. I have stated that children in EBD schools may need the support of various services and that each service will be planning intervention from the perspective of its own paradigm. Teachers meet emotional and behavioural difficulties in an educational context and within-child labels can produce low expectation of a teacher's ability to mediate change. Diagnostic and medical labels can be counterproductive as they locate a difficulty within a child and focus our attention on difficulty and impairment rather than need. The outcome of this can be schools that focus on treatment rather than teaching.

From a 'treatment' perspective, an EBD school becomes a community for damaged and disturbed children who will vent their anger and display deviant behaviour in order to exorcise their emotional disturbance. The school might see itself as a 'therapeutic community' and can become a place where the primary consideration is therapy and the curriculum is an afterthought.

Expectation of curriculum attainment, achievement and engagement should never become low because they have been superseded by the therapeutic concerns of 'healing' children who are deemed to be damaged. Children with emotional and behavioural difficulties can gain the therapeutic benefits of emotional 'recovery and development' by raising their self-esteem through achievement and attainment in the whole curriculum, which includes the National Curriculum. Learning that you can learn provides valuable therapy.

I do not reject therapeutic interventions and therapeutic perspectives, nor do I deny that certain children require them. In meeting learning needs we should gather multiple points of view before we design curriculum programmes. A blinkered and dogmatic rejection of models other than the educational one limits the possibility of educational progress for the pupils.

Managing a school entails full accountability. In a management position you cannot be accountable for some aspects of the school and not for others. A collegial and democratic style of management still requires someone to make the decisions. One influential decision concerns the implementation of a priority model for the school and the acceptance that the school will have to deal with some of the contradictions that arise when competing ideologies interact or clash. Balancing, restructuring or presenting contradictions for interpretation is not a new concept; it is the objective of some of the great works of drama, literature, art and music. A school should be courageous and creative in implementing its vision, and the main focus must be on educational outcomes – learning. This principle must apply to an EBD school.

Design a label

I remember a discussion I had with Dennis Goldthorpe, the inspirational head teacher of Alexandra School. Someone with a penchant for labels had asked us to describe the model that we had developed in the school. It was a model that had been implemented by all staff because every one of us had a commitment to teaching in the classroom. We talked of our emphasis on metacognition, our unswerving commitment to the curriculum, our focus on needs, and our acceptance that emotional recovery was important. We had deliberately developed an approach that contained some superficially contradictory ideologies. After much discussion, we decided that we were 'eclectic' and proud of it. However the outside world sometimes considers eclecticism to be another guise for accidentalism – success by fluke. This approach was not haphazard; it was meticulous eclecticism.

Teaching in an EBD school

How should we approach the teaching of pupils with emotional and behavioural difficulties? We can learn about the process of defining, planning and implementing the curriculum for children with learning difficulties from authors such as Sebba *et al.* (1995), Byers and Rose (1996) and Carpenter *et al.* (1996). There will be specific additional issues for EBD schools to consider such as curricular balance and the implementation of cross-curricular dimensions (Norwich 1990). A focus on teaching input and learning output is a suitable starting point to consider how we can meet the needs of such individuals in the process of teaching.

Input and output

When we are at the input stage of teaching we consider the critical factors that are relevant in relation to the child and the learning environment. Wedell (1995) proposes a model of 'compensatory interaction ' which analyses the interaction between such strengths and weaknesses. The application of this model to an EBD setting challenges teachers to investigate how social and personal expectations and aspirations can be become substantial determinants of learning need. A teacher has to consider the inhibitory or supportive nature of the interaction between internal and external resources in order to establish the positive opportunities for learning and progress.

A pupil in an EBD school brings an interactive balance of cognitive and emotional factors to this process, and this may cause them to reject any notion of themselves as learners and achievers. There may be multiple locations and causes of the emotional and behavioural learning difficulty. The issues of progress and recovery must be considered when planning to teach pupils who attend EBD schools. They are also important aspects of the curriculum for any child who experiences difficulty in learning.

Reading recovery or emotional recovery?

Reading can be a challenge to many pupils with learning difficulties and I shall take this aspect of the curriculum from which to provide an example of teaching issues in an EBD setting.

Godwin is four years behind his chronological reading age. His teacher accepts her professional responsibility to do something about it. Godwin may have a cognitive difficulty such as a poor short-term memory or pervasive attention difficulties. It may be that emotional factors determine his learning difficulty – previous negative experience of written text, fear of failure or the lack of emotional self-control to persevere. It is more likely that these factors interact. This makes the teaching of reading a challenge in that it may result in challenging behaviour. However, his need demands that he should be taught to read.

Emotional and behavioural recovery is the process of turning the child around; demonstrating that the child is a learner and can learn how to learn. This should be an explicit aspect of the curriculum that we provide for pupils with low self-esteem. Recovery does have a potentially uncomfortable medical connotation as it implies 'getting better', but in this context the element of getting better refers to his progress in reading. A teacher may have less control over the emotional aspects that the child brings to the teaching and learning process, but they gain increased power to make a change over time. The power to make a change should be shared with the pupil.

The whole curriculum, the National curriculum and the differentiated curriculum are major components of the learning environment. The curriculum provides us with evidence about what a child can do as well as what a child finds difficult. It is important to assert that the National Curriculum is not the whole curriculum and that the timetable is not the whole curriculum either. Figure 2.1 demonstrates how the pupil interacts with the curriculum and highlights the need for a link between 'learning and progress' and 'recovery and development' to be established. The intersecting circles illustrate the direction from which professionals approach the curriculum. The teacher's main focus is learning and progress, the psychologist approaches from the standpoint of recovery and development. The intersection will be larger or smaller in different real situations and gives prominence to cross-professional partnership.

The parents intersect with all of these professionals, and this can become a degrading and disempowering experience for them (Carpenter 1997). Trans-disciplinary practice has to become more family-centred so that the parents and the child have a central role in decision making (Doyle 1997).

This diagram indicates that the wholesale rejection of ideologies from competing models should not take place – it is not in the best interests of the child's learning needs. Teachers must be optimistic because teaching and

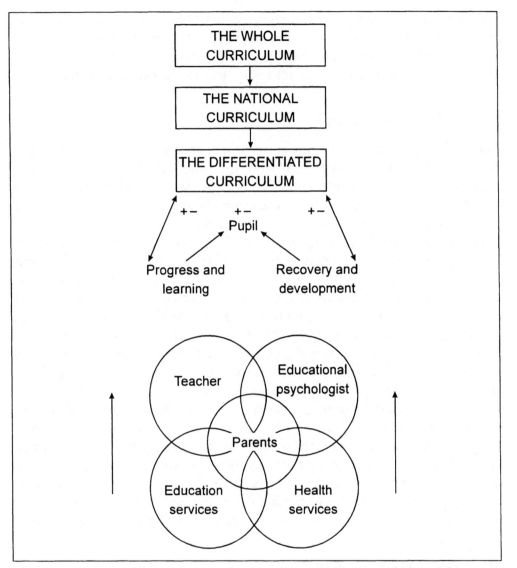

Figure 2.1   Curriculum routes and perspectives (O'Brien and Norwich)

assessment is a sequentially interactive process that enables us to gain insight into a child's cognitive and emotional map so that we can improve their self-concept and ability to learn.

Let us return to Godwin, the pupil with reading difficulties and associated emotional and behavioural difficulties. His teacher has established the location and causation of his learning difficulty and is aiming for progress in reading as well as progress in his emotional capacity to engage with a reading task in the future. Godwin can perform sophisticated task evasion, which might include threatening or abusive behaviour. It is clear that his challenging behaviour is a consequence not a causatory component of his learning difficulty – his behaviour is not independent of his learning. All of these factors have to be considered in relation to teaching input. Depending on the priority model of the school, Godwin could encounter a variety of scenarios. Here are two.

The responsive curriculum

Godwin's reading difficulty may superficially appear as a negative learning factor but the teacher starts from what the pupil can do – thus turning a negative learning factor into a positive teaching factor. Godwin can present with challenging behaviour, but suitably challenging work and specific and realistic praise can promote his positive behaviour.

The teacher provides a responsive teaching environment, which has an implicit and sensitive acceptance of Godwin's difficulty. It also has sufficient flexibility to respond to any emerging need as it arises. The teacher establishes Godwin's interests and sets an age-appropriate reading task that does not humiliate him and has meaning for him. Godwin is made aware of the teaching aim and his own learning goal. He is told that his teacher expects him to achieve it – although it might appear difficult to do so when he first attempts the task. He talks with the teacher about the reason for improving his reading skills. What was a potentially negative situation is now a potentially positive one.

As Godwin makes progress the teacher carefully assesses the cognitive and emotional output of teaching and involves the pupil in self-assessment too. Godwin is listened to respectfully when he talks about his progress, even when he appears very angry or very negative. After each step of learning, he is motivated to approach the next stage. The teacher's main emphasis is on learning progression but 'recovery and development' is also considered as an outcome of engaging in a differentiated curriculum and responsive teaching.

The 'hit and run' curriculum

Godwin is in a different school. The school sees him as damaged and disturbed and has built time-out into its everyday practice. There is no whole-school overview on its use but it involves leaving the classroom when you are upset so that you can choose a therapeutic activity: time in a soft play room, snooker, or collecting a large ball that you can punch or kick to release your anger. Angry pupils may also choose alternative activities if the set task increases their anger and results in abusive and threatening behaviour.

Godwin arrives in class, and it is time to read. He thinks it will be difficult so he performs his anxieties about reading through his behaviour – he begins swearing and kicking his chair. Godwin is in 'set-out-to-get-out' mode. The teacher will obviously not accept this behaviour and informs Godwin that he must be very angry to behave like this. Godwin's task rage needs resolving so he is given permission to leave, unsupervised and he makes his way to the snooker room. Within a short period of time Godwin has calmed down substantially. This is adopted as a regular strategy to help Godwin to control his anger.

In this scenario there is an emphasis on emotional recovery. Godwin has calmed down, and this will have met a goal related to recovery. However, this misses the point. Godwin is attending a school but he is not learning how to read. It could be argued that in a 'hit and run' scenario, time-out is not just opt-out, it is whole-school cop-out. Whilst these scenarios may appear to be caricatures, they are not impossible in the current picture of national EBD provision.

An EBD school has to adopt an eclectic approach to the management of teaching and learning with the main emphasis placed on raising a child's self-concept as a learner, and as a person, through whole curriculum achievement and attainment. In aiming to adopt a pure and uncontaminated model, a school can leave some teachers with no option but to place an over-emphasis on therapy. An EBD school that adheres to one model – for example, a singularly psychodynamic approach, however diluted it might be – assumes that all emotional and behavioural difficulties require the same response. It also assumes that each member of staff has a coherent understanding of psychodynamic theory. Its pragmatic and inflexible stance compromises its ability to be fully responsive to individual pupil needs. It also rejects some of the common needs that pupils share with peers who attend mainstream school. Its focus on the distinct needs of children make it unaccountable to the holistic learning requirements of an individual child.

The result is an institutional imbalance where emotional and behavioural recovery becomes the major priority of a school. This particular emphasis might encourage a school to redefine itself as 'a therapeutic community' when it does not have the qualified staff to support such a claim. This transforms the qualified teacher into an unqualified therapist and will be to the detriment of continuity, progress, and achievement through the curriculum. The mindless adherence to such a model sells the pupils short.

Cautionary tales

In describing an approach to teaching children with emotional and behavioural difficulties, I have affirmed the role of the teacher as a pedagogue. A colleague once explained to me why the job of being a teacher was no longer the job that she signed up for many years ago. She described a new role where teachers were becoming multifaceted professionals – teacher, social worker, therapist, counsellor, police officer, psychologist and replacement parent, all rolled into one. She may have been correct in describing some of the operational aspects of the role of a teacher but fundamentally she was incorrect.

It is important to emphasise that teachers are trained as *teachers* and undertake professional development to improve their teaching. Our skills should relate to the understanding and implementation of the process of teaching and learning. We may do this through a variety of means including supporting children through crisis, demonstrating that there are adults that can be trusted, considering psychological theories, setting and implementing consistent boundaries for behaviour and providing for spiritual and moral growth. This does not mean that we have stopped being teachers and that our expertise should be detached from teaching and learning. We are not trained members of the other professions that she described and we should not pretend to be so.

Teaching is not acting

When I was training to be a teacher, I remember a lecturer telling us that although we thought we were teachers, in fact we were not – we were actors. At first I thought this was a philosophical joke. 'Teaching is acting and the best teachers are actors,' he continued. I cannot accept this because acting is an illusory process where an audience is convinced that the actor is somebody other than their real self. Through pretence, the audience is enticed into believing that the actor possesses the personality, characteristics and aspirations of someone else. When I intervene in a situation where a child is presenting severely violent or self-injurious behaviour, I adopt certain strategies. These approaches inform the child that I am not a threat nor am I threatened and that I can help them to regain self-control. This is not acting; it is applying the skills that I have developed as a teacher. I am not pretending to be someone different; I am still me.

The responsive relationship that a teacher builds with a child will be shattered if, in a child's most distressing times such as moments of severe challenging behaviour, the teacher becomes a completely different person. Teaching may involve many elements of performance, but it not acting. 'The best teachers are actors' is a false and hazardous assumption.

Inspection week can become a time when teaching is transformed into acting, and this can have a detrimental effect in a special school where challenging behaviour is prevalent. The illusory veil of acting can aim to camouflage the reason why the children attend a special school. If a child is placed in a special school because of learning needs that present as challenging behaviour, it is to be expected that during inspection there will be evidence of their needs and difficulties. The school should accept this and provide evidence of planned intervention, consistency of approach and documentation of progress. It should justify the distinct provision that is matched to the child's needs. The best teachers adopt preventative strategies and deploy skills that defuse challenging behaviour. They should not feel pressurised into acting as if challenging behaviour does not, and never has, existed in their special school. The transformation of a school by a sudden influx of plants and flowers is another pre-inspection camouflage strategy – it is the fertility of the curriculum and the blossoming of new learning that should really be on display.

Role dilemma

The problem of role duality can seriously affect our perception of role reality. Chuang Tzu, the Chinese philosopher, was one of the earliest exponents of Taoism. 'Tzu' is a title that means 'master' and signifies his elevation as a model teacher. His allegorical style was used to communicate his views on the expansion and liberation of the individual mind. He adopted a witty and subversive teaching style.

Chuang Tzu tells us how he fell asleep one evening. He dreamed that he was a butterfly, fluttering about in a state of release and enjoyment. The butterfly did not know it was Chuang Tzu; it thought it was a butterfly. Suddenly, he awoke with a start and instantly became Chuang Tzu again – or did he? He was now tortured by the fact that he did not know whether he was Chuang Tzu who had dreamed he was a butterfly, or whether he was a butterfly dreaming that he was Chuang Tzu.

This role dilemma had a detrimental affect on his ability to teach. He attempted to come to terms with his own internal confusion, but was never absolutely certain if he was a butterfly or a teacher. So, the next time you begin to think that you are a social worker, a counsellor, a therapist, or even a butterfly – be warned!

The role of differentiation

Differentiation is an active process through which a teacher can communicate to a child that they are recognised and valued. Differentiated resources should reflect diversity of learning style, and teaching should recognise common, distinct and individual needs. The differentiated curriculum cannot depend solely on the intuitive or charismatic teacher. Differentiation has to be grounded

Every child can learn

Every teacher can learn

Learning is a dynamic process which requires
mutual responsivity

Progress will be expected, recognised and rewarded

Every child is entitled to high quality education

Environments and people can change

Figure 2.2   Six principles for active differentiation

in principles that inform teaching style and ensure curriculum responsivity. In this way children who may present challenging behaviour feel that the curriculum and the teacher are saying 'I accept you. I like you. I know what you can do, and I expect you to make progress.'

Figure 2.2 presents six principles that promote differentiation as an interactive process for all children. The expectation is that every pupil is capable of learning and that the tools and process of differentiation provide every teacher with the opportunity to learn. The collaborative nature of a differentiated learning environment must not be overlooked – children can learn with each other and from each other, and the learning network increases when teachers are added to this interactive partnership. There is high expectation that progress will be expected and planned for and that the teacher will recognise and reward progress. Progress should start from the child's baseline, have clear steps and should acknowledge the achievement of a 'personal best'. In a differentiated environment a learner should never feel marginalised, anonymous or invisible. A commitment to believing that environments and people can change for the better makes the education of all children a reality.

The six principles are complemented by six methods which are shown in Figure 2.3.

Differentiation as communication

Responsive and positive mutual communication is the lifeblood of differentiation. In an effectively differentiated learning environment children and teachers should be able to articulate why a task is taking place. The response

Method	Key word
Task	Curriculum
Resource	Choice
Outcome	Confidence
Presentation	Flexibility
Organisation	Collaboration
Environment	Alterability

Figure 2.3   Six methods of active differentiation

from the child should move beyond 'I'm doing it because Miss asked me to.' A child's learning difficulty should not prevent high expectation of potential achievement and attainment, and therefore a differentiated environment must communicate that learning involves a process as well as a product.

The 'process' of learning is often given a high priority for children who experience learning difficulties. We must ensure that, in this context, 'valuing learning as a process' is not teacher-code for saying that we do not expect too much in terms of product. Of course many children with learning difficulties will not achieve to norm-referenced standards of attainment relating to chronological age, but differentiation enables us to discover what they can do and can enable them to achieve.

A national norm-referenced framework would indicate that a child with PMLD is a low attainer. To colleagues in special education, this description is completely absurd, because recognising each achievement and attainment has to take into account the factors that each learner brings to a task. Consequently a child with PMLD can be described as a 'high attainer' whenever they demonstrate that they are learning something new within their own individual context.

To ensure curriculum dynamism, teachers must consider differentiation of the curriculum within the child's legislated entitlement to curricular provision that is broad, balanced, relevant and differentiated. A school will make decisions about balance and breadth and the time required for these curriculum conditions to exist. A curriculum audit can monitor whether breadth and balance will be achieved over one term, two terms, or one year. Issues of relevance will be considered in relation to individual and common needs and the whole curriculum will place an additional focus on the distinct needs of the pupils in the particular school. The curriculum must be differentiated so that the teaching aim can be matched to the learning need.

Differentiation as a process and a tool

Differentiation requires teachers to consider the complex process and tools of curriculum access. The starting point for differentiation must be a consideration of the three categories of need (Figure 1.2). Teachers will be aware that they have to consider needs that are common to all children. There will also be distinct needs that may apply to groups of children and these could include those needs that are currently described as special educational needs. Finally, there will be specific individual needs that apply to each particular child. In this way the teacher must see the class as a whole group, as multiple combinations of children and as a complete set of unique individuals. This highlights the complexities of providing a differentiated environment.

Differentiation is not only the complex creative task of the planning, preparation, management and development of learning resources that will provide a match between the learner and the curriculum. It is also the complex intellectual process of conceptualising common human needs and emerging group and individual needs, and employing sensitive and responsive teaching. The process of differentiation must concern itself with individual learning styles and their place within collective learning styles; it is far more complex than the slight adaptation of a task or the expectation of a different outcome from the same task. It is an experimental and creative process that must allow pupils and teachers to take risks in an atmosphere where a mistake is accepted as part of the process of learning.

It cannot be assumed that the process of differentiation will take place simply because it appears as a legislative entitlement. Providing a differentiated learning environment is relative to the type of school in which it takes place. There are difficulties for a secondary school teacher who teaches twelve different form groups per week and has the responsibility of seeing the children as individuals and not just a homogeneous group called 5B – to gain insight into the learning needs of hundreds of children will take time. Similarly, a teacher working within a special school with a culture of individualised teaching and curriculum objectives must ensure that a focus on meeting individual needs does not result in a child consistently working on their own. Being near other children in an inclusive setting, for example sitting at the same table as others, is not an indicator that you are involved in inclusive learning. The primary or special school subject coordinator and the high school head of department should be expected to have a wider perspective on differentiation. They should not only be able to justify how their curriculum area is meeting particular individual needs but also how it meets needs that are common to all children. Each curriculum area must incorporate the common needs of children and consequently those with curriculum area responsibility must be aware of what their subject offers to a child's spiritual, moral, social and cultural development.

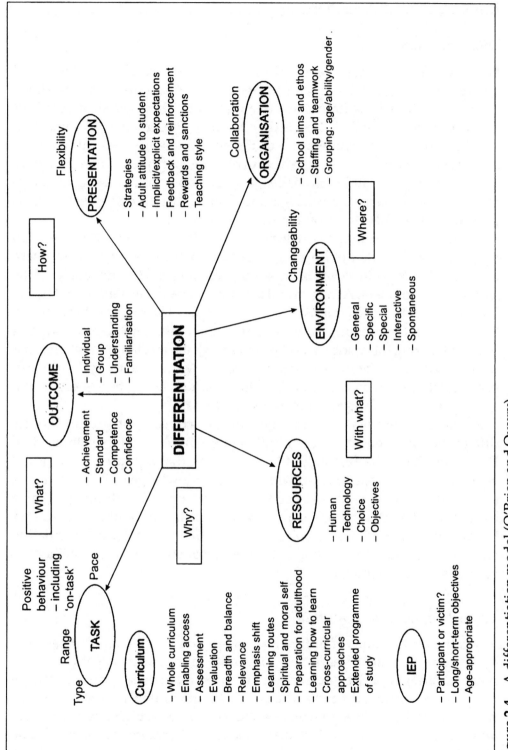

Figure 2.4 A differentiation model (O'Brien and Ouvry)

Differentiation in action

Figure 2.4 demonstrates an enquiry-process model for differentiation. Carol Ouvry and I designed it for use in a range of special schools. It has since been used successfully by staff in mainstream schools. There are six methods of active differentiation: Task, Resources, Outcome, Presentation, Organisation and Environment. Consideration of the environment is critical for those colleagues in special schools who have to differentiate the environment before they can even get a child with challenging behaviour to sit down or attend to any task. Some mainstream colleagues are finding that the movement towards inclusion has led them to encounter such children too.

The teacher is encouraged to consider critical features of the differentiation method – the flexibility of learning presentation, the extent to which collaborative methods are involved in organising learning and the alterability of the learning environment. Access in and around this model is determined by the questions that the teacher is asking – for example, 'How can I differentiate?' 'What am I differentiating?' and 'Why am I differentiating?' I would suggest that before using the model, a teacher should ask the most important question of all – 'What is the point of doing this piece of work or activity?' The entry point is determined by your answer to this question. It will be a question that the pupils will be asking and it requires a reply.

A teacher might want to promote a constructivist approach and to use differentiation to ensure that a pupil is more involved in their Individual Education Plan. The IEP should be something that a pupil is part of, not something being done to them without their knowledge of its existence. A starting point might relate to a need to prepare pupils for adulthood. It may be that a differentiated task is presented in order to monitor the on-task behaviour of a child. Being able to identify the reason for differentiating enables the teacher to decide upon the method or combination of methods to employ when differentiating.

Equality of learning opportunity

When the complexities of differentiation are looked at in detail, it becomes evident that equality of learning opportunity cannot mean equality of treatment. A colleague once expressed concern to me about a child with a statement of special educational needs who had been integrated into his class in a mainstream school. His argument was that there were thirty children in the class and this particular lesson lasted for one hour therefore in terms of equal opportunity the equation was perfect – each child should be allocated two minutes of teacher time per lesson. The child with the statement was taking up a far greater allocation of teacher time and this was considered to be an example of where it was not possible to achieve equal opportunities for all. Of course, this colleague was not talking about equal opportunity at all; he was referring to equal treatment. We do not have equality of learning capability so we cannot expect to have equal treatment – some children will need more input during the stages of the learning process than others. A differentiated environment makes equality of learning opportunity possible. It should always be accompanied by equality of learning dignity.

This interaction with my colleague encapsulated the debate about diversity and difference. I propose that in order to celebrate diversity and difference we must be able to be precise about individuality by starting with commonality. The 'common, distinct, individual' pathway to identifying needs offers the information that brings progressive clarity to the process of differentiation.

Teaching to the middle – is it teach and hope?

The model as illustrated in Figure 2.4 aims to support colleagues who feel overwhelmed by learning needs or learning difficulties and who develop 'teaching to the middle' as their response. In the reality of the busy classroom this can mean an awareness and understanding of the needs of the children but an anxiety about the lack of the time or resources to be able to meet them – a potentially soul-destroying reality for someone teaching a class of thirty-five children. The teacher develops work that will meet the majority of needs and then makes an effort to extend the more able and support those who are experiencing difficulties.

Teaching to the middle can also describe a 'teach and hope' model, where the teaching takes place and the teacher hopes that the majority of children will learn. The aim is to produce an increase in the mean level of attainment – an important outcome under the pressure of a market-driven ideology that publishes league tables of attainment. This aim has a detrimental effect on the pupils with special educational needs and when it creates a general minimum standard, it produces low levels of achievement for the most able pupils (Eyre 1997). Every pupil needs challenging tasks and the extension of learning has to involve an increase in the quality of a new task rather than an increase in the quantity of the same task. Task repetition might provide short-term practice or revision but as a consistent strategy to provide new learning it will only promote a cult of mediocrity.

Other teachers who are overwhelmed by learning needs aim to teach at the extremes in an attempt to reduce class variance. In this approach those pupils who are 'in the middle' might spend a vast proportion of their time involved in curriculum cruising. These children may be passive in their reaction to cruising time and might include a large proportion of children who are insultingly categorised by the term 'average'. An aim to teach at the extremes of need does a great disservice to such children particularly when self-fulfilling prophecy takes its grip and 'average' becomes 'anonymous'. An analytical approach to differentiation should prevent this taking place, although it is wholly unrealistic to expect every child to be experiencing a suitably differentiated learning experience every single time that they engage with the curriculum.

The exit question from the model should lead to an evaluation of the joint learning that has taken place. The teacher should ask 'What have the pupils learnt and what have I learnt?' If these questions cannot be answered then the teacher needs to return to explore new methods of differentiation that will provide the answers.

Differentiation – painting the picture

If we were able to spend some time inside a child's head I am sure that we would find learning to be a very noisy and colourful process. For most children there are few occasions when learning is smooth, balanced, compartmentalised and rhythmical – like a Mondrian painting. The reality is that learning is more likely to be loud, chaotic, syncopated and explosive – less like Mondrian, more like Kandinsky. Learning is a noisy and risky business and differentiation should aim to reduce the sound of cognitive dissonance. Without differentiation we present all children with the curriculum version of 'still life'.

Chapter 3

The whole child requires whole learning: providing spiritual development

Promoting positive behaviour takes place within the context of the whole child, the whole school and the broad aims of education – it cannot happen in isolation. The 1988 Education Reform Act places education within the context of the spiritual, moral, social, cultural, mental and physical development of pupils and of society. If all children are equally entitled to a high standard of education then every pupil in every school has the right to an education that plans for development in these areas. Their education will also contribute to the development of society. The 1992 Education (Schools) Act required OFSTED to report on pupils' spiritual, moral, social and cultural development as part of its inspection framework and schools had to identify how they were providing for such development.

Defining spirituality

The National Curriculum Council published a discussion paper in 1993 that provided guidance for schools in defining what spiritual and moral development means in a school setting. It listed examples of how development could take place. This paper defines spirituality in terms of relationships with others and, where relevant, with God. It also refers to a search for meaning and purpose and highlights the universal quest to understand our individual identity. A number of aspects of spiritual development are put forward and these include:

- a sense of awe, wonder and mystery
- a search for meaning and purpose
- feelings and emotions
- self-knowledge
- beliefs – these beliefs need not necessarily be related to a religious belief system.

Spirituality is seen as 'Something fundamental in the human condition which is not necessarily experienced through the physical senses and/or expressed through everyday language' (NCC 1993, p. 3).

This guidance indicates how a school might begin to quantify the area of spiritual development and provides an insight into how pupils might encounter it. Further guidance has been made available (SCAA 1995, 1996) which reinforces the position that spiritual development is fundamental to other areas of learning. The OFSTED framework for inspection emphasises that the development of a pupil's insight into their own existence requires us to take a view of spirituality that is broader than one defined by the parameters of a religious faith.

With such guidance available to us, why is it that some schools find spiritual development an area where they cannot justify what they are doing, how they are doing it, and the difference that it is making? Inspection reports show that some schools provide spectacular spiritual development while others do not seem to have grasped how it can be done or are not aware of how what they are already doing fits into a framework for spiritual development. Her Majesty's Chief Inspector of Schools states in his most recent annual report (OFSTED 1997) that the majority of schools have well established aims for spiritual, moral, social and cultural development. The need to put all of these areas of development into practice causes some consternation: 'Pupils' spiritual development, however, remains problematic for most schools and this is often the least satisfactory of the four areas of development.' (p. 25)

The concept of spiritual development in an educational setting requires deconstruction and reconstruction of meaning so that all teachers can be aware of its relevance to them in their daily work.

I shall concentrate mainly on the area of spiritual development although I accept that there is a complex interplay between all four areas of development, particularly spiritual and moral. They interact with each other in a manner which causes them to be both separate and integrated. In relation to the management of teaching and learning, I have suggested that an effective starting point would be to consider teaching input and learning output. In applying the same approach to spiritual development, it has to be accepted that a spiritual input does not necessarily result in a moral output.

Teachers' interpretation of 'spiritual'

The term 'spiritual' conjures up a variety of personal responses from adults working in education. They may associate it solely with religious belief and tradition and this causes difficulties. Those who have had negative formative experiences of religious faith may have a dismissive or aggressive response to the idea that schools should be required to promote spiritual development. Those with a commitment to a faith may perceive spirituality to be directly associated with one specific set of religious beliefs, doctrines and practices.

Others may perceive the term to mean something ethereal, nebulous and unrelated to a view of their role as a transmitter of knowledge and facts. Spirituality contains the word 'spirit' and carries intense religious symbolism for many people. In a discussion about spirituality we would expect to talk about children in terms of their worth, consciousness, potential, nature and human essence and we will enquire about ideas of ultimate truth and reality.

Some teachers will not see a link between such concepts and their own curriculum responsibilities and classroom practice. It is likely that these colleagues will believe that spirituality belongs within the remit of the staff responsible for Religious Education (RE) or Personal and Social Education (PSE). For example, a secondary school geography teacher may wonder if spiritual education can ever form part of her curriculum. The early years teacher may feel the same about his curriculum.

Once a definition is agreed, responsibility can be shared. Any definition should begin by emphasising that the child has an entitlement to a sense of holistic well being. Spiritual development must be an inclusive concept because it asserts the right of every child to actively participate in education and not to be a passive recipient of it. A commitment to spiritual inclusivity should never diminish because of a person's cognitive abilities or stage of development. The philosophical commitment to the educability of all children entitles each child to receive teaching that will allow them to experience and gain an insight into their own unique existence. It will also enable them to understand the value of their existence in relation to others.

Spiritual experience or spiritual development?

I once took a group of children, who were labelled as having emotional and behavioural difficulties, to a Gurdwara. We sat below the Guru Granth Sahib and heard the Granthi chanting. The children sat silently and listened intently to what was being said. Only one of the children understood Punjabi but all of them seemed to understand and experience the universal language of spirituality. Spirituality and learning was the issue, not emotional and be-havioural difficulties. Some days later, the same group of children was painting when one of them called me over to her work. She was marvelling at the colour blue that she had mixed. This eight-year-old girl was enquiring about the 'blueness' of the colour blue. Moreover, she was expecting a response from me! On another occasion, a different child asked a colleague of mine 'What does red look like from the back?' These examples of reflective enquiry are spiritual experiences. Spiritual experiences can be planned for and a responsive environment will encourage them to take place and to be valued.

I have deliberately described these two incidents as spiritual 'experience'. Children have been involved in shared or personal engagement and reflection. As a teacher, I may have provided powerful spiritual experiences but I cannot be certain that I have provided spiritual *development*. The term 'development' has an implicit notion of change, progress, and learning. An 'experience', and an individual's involvement in it, may be transient and might not necessarily result in planned or assessed growth and change. In providing for development we are promoting a concept of spiritual learning within an educational context. This raises a further question. Are teachers being asked to establish a spiritual baseline for each child? If so, this appears to remove spirituality from the realms of transcendence and into familiar curriculum areas that can be assessed and evaluated. If we are expected to assess spiritual development within the National Curriculum we must remove ourselves from the paradigm of linear continuity and progression and establish a new conceptual framework for the expansive dimensions of spiritual progress. Spiritual needs should not be restrained and restricted by the National Curriculum.

These are some of the many issues involved in developing a consensus about spiritual development in an educational context. In this book I have argued that a school can manage learning most effectively by adopting a pluralistic and eclectic approach. The same is required when defining spiritual development and provision in a school – it must accommodate common perspectives from a variety of traditions including those that are religious, humanistic or atheistic. Clearly, spiritual development is a learning issue and the education system has been given the responsibility of providing for the spiritual development of individuals and society.

Spiritual needs

Earlier in this book, I proposed that the process for identifying individuality should begin by identifying commonality. In special education this prevents staff from becoming overwhelmed by obvious individual differences to the detriment of recognising human similarities. We must similarly begin by establishing the spiritual common ground before we can identify individual spiritual needs.

Schools should aim to meet common, distinct and individual learning needs in an educational context (see Figure 1.2). Spiritual development is a statutory component of this context and we must begin to consider spiritual needs as learning needs and investigate how they can be met in our schools. Figure 3.1 illustrates how spiritual needs can be met within an educational context.

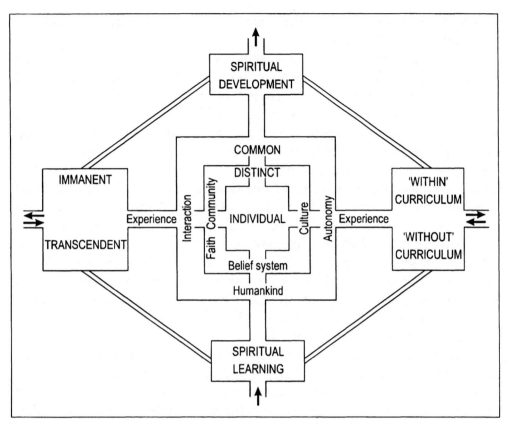

Figure 3.1 Meeting spiritual needs in a school setting

Common spiritual needs

The broader psychosocial aspects of spiritual development can be identified within this category. The fundamental aims of education encompass the spiritual needs of all children and thus a school should develop its ability to enable a child to interpret her or his experiences of the world around them. My contention is that in order to begin to develop a concept of personhood, you have to understand and learn that you are a person. All of our inter-actions with children should emphasise their personhood and their potential to be autonomous. We should assert their right to make choices, express preferences and to interact critically with their environment. We can show the child that she or he is a person of worth by the nature of our attitudes and interactions and the dignity that we afford to them. In this way, children gain an insight into the human condition and an awareness of the impact of their own existence within an integrated, pluralistic and democratic society. Education should not concern itself with preparing children *for* their entry into society; it should be preparing them to understand their current and future significance as *part of* society.

When we provide opportunities that will expand the individual consciousness of a child we are teaching them that they are different from all other living entities around them. Their consciousness of 'being' leads to an understanding of individuality. Being alive endows you with rights and value as an individual. It also identifies needs such as finding a purpose in what you are doing, the need to be loved, the need for interactive communication, the need to be safe and the need to belong. These needs could be described as some of the basic, common spiritual needs of humankind. Consciousness of 'self' empowers a child to determine what they want and need without the intervention of others, and to develop an interest in the critical changes that they can make to their own environment.

Promoting self-advocacy (Sandow and Garner 1995) is one way in which a school can provide for spiritual development. Schools should remain cognisant of the need to adopt a variety of interactive teaching styles (McGee *et al.* 1987; Nind and Hewett 1994) in order to involve pupils in the development and direction of their own learning routes.

A school that can define common needs in this way does not need to be anxious in justifying how it promotes spiritual development. The mutuality involved in an interactive relationship between a learner and a teacher is a basis for spiritual development. Developing systems that offer responsibility or that give the children a voice that is actively heard are also examples of how a school can provide for their common spiritual development. The acknowledgement of a child when we pass them in a busy school corridor, either by a smile, eye contact, or by greeting them verbally, makes a contribution to their spiritual development.

Distinct spiritual needs

Having considered the wider needs of a person within society we can begin to investigate the spiritual needs of children within a school setting. These needs will be relative to the type of school, its ethos, and the nature of the children who are educated within it. I have emphasised that common needs will relate to the self in a wider social setting and I shall now suggest that distinct spiritual needs relate to the setting and context that a school provides. The school should emphasise the role of individuality within a learning community composed of children and adults who have the propensity for spiritual growth.

A school creates and develops its own consciousness, and this will involve a moral code of shared values that comply with an accepted notion of social morality. The link between spiritual, moral, social and cultural development is significant at the point of analysing intended and unintended components of school consciousness. The collective consciousness of a school, its collective meanings, understandings, values, ideologies and aspirations is constructed in a political, cultural, religious and social context. A school does not want to produce children who are driven by an autonomous desire for ego gratification that is destructive to individuals, their peers, or to society. It cannot afford to allow each child to function solely on personal identity and to reject the concept of citizenship inherent in a notion of social self. Rational social autonomy creates the framework from which the school can provide individual autonomy that will liberate its children. School collective identity can ascribe a deeper meaning to the child's personal and social identity.

Beyond tolerance

A cohesive collective consciousness will be articulated through the school aims and the methods by which they are implemented. Most importantly, aims should be driven by an agreed concept of what is of *worth* to the school community. Clarity about collective worth can enable teachers to mediate experiences, provide a positive ethos, and promote individual and communal growth. I have seen many school mission statements and aims that herald 'tolerance' as a virtuous element of their collective consciousness. This could be construed as heralding tolerance as an optimal state of mind and action for meeting distinct spiritual needs. However, this is based on the supposition that each individual has an entitlement to be who they are, and that all individuals must learn to tolerate each other. Not only does the concept of tolerance suggest a distance in a relationship; it also implies a detached sense of value-judgement.

Relationships that promote spiritual development should be based on respect. I do not consider tolerance to be an embodiment of respect because it contains so many ambiguous messages about diversity. In a community that sees a direct link between learning and spiritual development, the word 'tolerated' needs to be replaced by 'understood'. Spiritual progress is limited by a lack of the desire to understand and be understood.

Particular groups

Some children feel the pain of harbouring the secret of being abused and experience the fear of not knowing if there are any adults that they can trust. They may blame themselves as a person, they might present self-injurious behaviour or they may display instrumental violence towards others. This is one example of an area where a school must incorporate the experiences and spiritual needs of its children into its definition of collective worth. A behaviour policy that is based on respectful intervention promotes the individual and collective spiritual development of the pupil. The school community also develops because it offers the pupils increasing responsibility to participate in changing their own behaviour.

The spiritual development of children with PMLD is not an enigma. A teacher who strives to implement a responsive environment (Ware 1996) will be in a position to promote the spiritual development of a child with PMLD. A progressive increase in contingency awareness (Ware 1994) may be used as an indicator of spiritual development for such children. Once a child can direct their own quality of life, rather than having it directed for them, their world and their impact upon it can evolve and extend. The role of technology in enabling spiritual development should not be overlooked.

The subject-driven force behind the National Curriculum has created a dilemma for those teachers who believe that a needs-led curriculum is more relevant for pupils with PMLD. The issue here is that whatever a child is learning, it has to be relevant to the needs of that child. If the curriculum is not meeting the learning needs of a child then it limits their potential for spiritual development. Pupils with PMLD should not have their spiritual needs abandoned due to curriculum fragmentation and irrelevance. Adopting an approach of teaching *through* National Curriculum subjects, as well as *in* them (Ouvry and Saunders 1996), provides a curriculum framework that will meet the distinct spiritual needs of those pupils with PMLD.

Spiritual development in its collective educational setting encompasses the distinct needs of children who belong to faith communities and thus cannot be devoid of social, cultural and political influence. Political ideology and the concept of national spirituality can suppress the spiritual development of children who experience learning difficulties. For example, by imposing market forces as the axiom of the education system, a national spiritual identity will place its highest regard on individuals who can contribute to a competitive national and global business economy. Market-force education can reinforce a dislocated and hopeless image of disability and learning difficulty. It also has a negative effect upon the social expectation of the potential for people with learning difficulties to become emancipated adults.

Individual spiritual needs

Individual spiritual needs are particular, relative and idiosyncratic. They will exist in different contexts and at different times and will be directly related to a person's own unique human experience. In a school setting it is important to accept that a child's own individual spiritual needs are defined by the experiential framework of the child and not defined by a teacher. The potential for individual spiritual development has to be seen as something that is an organic element of the learning process. A teacher should never believe that any child has reached their full potential.

When a teacher slips into auto-teacher mode this can inhibit the development of a child's individual spiritual needs. This mode prompts the teacher to intervene and describe a child's experience from a teacher perspective. 'I know just how you feel.' or 'What you are trying to say is . . . .' could be precursors to slipping into this mode. The teacher responds to the desire to project their professional and personal knowledge and perceptions onto a child's interpretation of their own experience. Consequently, the experiences of the pupil are processed and made meaningful within the teacher's terms of reference, not the pupil's. Spiritual insight and the ability to reflect do not necessarily follow a chronological progression and it has to be affirmed that every child has the potential to provide for the spiritual development of adults.

In meeting individual spiritual needs we encourage a child to reflect on what it is that makes them unique. Self-awareness involves learning about yourself and what you like and dislike. Self-knowledge has a direct effect on your thoughts, responses and behaviour. It involves the development of individual curiosity, as well as reflection on who you are and how you feel about yourself. At times, it can involve the potentially painful experience of metaphysical and existential self-interrogation (Sartre 1943), when the child becomes concerned that the links between being and destiny are fragile and synthetic.

Children with emotional and behavioural difficulties may have a negative self-image, and feel that whatever they do, it can never be right. Demonstrating to a child that they can learn and achieve is part of the provision a school makes for individual spiritual development. Enabling a child to demonstrate increased self-esteem is a method of assessing their spiritual development. Children who live in a state of enforced self-sufficiency or those forced to deal with the invasion, victimisation, pain, and guilt brought on by abuse, deserve a school that will respond to their individual spiritual needs. Self-awareness can be explored through internal and external reflection. In a school system where we encourage pupils to self-assess and self-differentiate, we must be able to develop approaches that challenge and encourage pupils to self-transcend.

Individual contexts

Individual spiritual needs are also situational and relative to individual development. As the self develops different spiritual needs emerge. Young children often search for trust in their relationships with others. As they reach adolescence they move beyond basic trust and begin to question the value and meaning of relationships (Narayanasamy 1997). This must be taken into account when dealing with situations that highlight a child's individual needs – such as how a child responds to bereavement.

A school must consider how a child will receive spiritual support when returning to school after a family bereavement. A whole-school response to situations involving grief and bereavement should be in place. The school has a significant role in helping the child cope with their grief (Dyregrov 1991). It is too important to be left to chance. The inability of the school to respond to these needs can devalue the experience of the child and the significance of the event. The school should not exclusively consider the child's needs when bereavement occurs, it should also consider the distinct needs of the learning community. Bereavement also highlights the needs of teachers. Teachers who work with children who are life-threatened will recognise the need for the school to offer professional support to them in preparing for the loss of a child.

The complex individual reactions of children who are depressed, stressed or traumatised (Yule 1991) should also be seen in a spiritual context by schools.

Each individual child exists within a spiritual context. An ex-colleague of mine was concerned that a child in her class was suddenly starting to develop a form of stereotypy in his behaviour. He was regularly rubbing his feet and ankles and flapping his ears. This was reducing his ability to participate in curriculum activities. There seemed to be no specific reason for the sudden onset of this frequent behaviour. We spoke with his parents and discovered that he had recently attended the mosque. He was performing his own inter-pretation of the actions of 'wudhu' that are required when washing before prayer. What had presented as low level challenging behaviour, was an important step in his spiritual development. The school was able to introduce a more positive and relevant setting in which the behaviour could occur.

The consideration of the three categories of spiritual need demonstrates that spirituality is far more than just 'awe and wonder' and that it is not bound by the restrictions of formal religious practice. I have aimed to provide a more concrete and less nebulous definition of spiritual development and indicate that it can be planned for, identified and assessed. The issue of assessment is extremely complex and will be compounded by instances such as a child with PMLD who self-injures. Is this a significant early step on their spiritual path, where they begin explore the notion of being alive by sensory stimulation that is self-injurious?

Schools should have the confidence to document how they are meeting the spiritual needs of the children while accepting that all categories of need may not be met at the same time. Spiritual development concerns itself with the whole child and their whole experience. It will occur through and beyond the differentiated curriculum in a range and breadth of immanent and trans-cendent experiences.

Whose job is it anyway?

I have asserted that spiritual development occurs 'within' and 'without' the curriculum, so whose responsibility is it? Someone must have responsibility, because poor provision for spiritual development can be a factor that influences a decision for a school to be placed under 'special measures' by an inspection team. Recently, I was being shown around a friend's school, when I saw the figure of an adolescent boy, trying to look inconspicuous, at the end of a large corridor. He began to shuffle about and stare inquisitively at a blank wall, as if to suggest that there was a legitimate purpose for him being out of class in the middle of a lesson. The teacher who was showing me around asked him: 'Who are you and what are you doing here?' These questions have fundamental and universal spiritual significance and in a different context this would have been the perfect opening to the ultimate conversation. This insightful questioning made me wonder if I was in the company of a 'teacher in charge of spirituality'.

I have presented an argument that any progress in a child's learning state is an indication of spiritual progress. Teaching children to develop an incremental awareness of what is within and beyond their own unique experience is a learning process, and must become the responsibility of every teacher. This does not call for wholesale reform of our current curricular provision. It will call upon some schools to produce a change in their perception and emphasis in how they are providing for spiritual development. We can plan for spiritual development, but must also be flexible enough to 'seize the moment' when it occurs. A sense of 'mysterium, tremendum et fascinans' (Otto 1950) can occur in any experience that the school intends, or does not intend, to provide and it is often referred to as 'awe and wonder'. Awe and wonder are present not only in those amazing moments of intense spiritual insight, they are also implicit in the paradoxes and ambiguities of life. Opportunities to listen, to be still, to contemplate, and to evaluate are vital components in this process.

Spirituality in the curriculum

The maths lesson about patterns and sequential relationships is providing for a child's spiritual development. Activities that enable children to attribute sense and meaning to the world around them provide for spiritual development. A geography teacher can do this through a lesson about the local environment or changes in settlement. The aesthetic subjects can provide a child with the chance for self-expression and the creative development of their consciousness. They can also produce moments of wonder when a child finds it hard to believe that they have cultivated the skills to be so creative.

The early years teacher, who offers a variety of contexts in which children can play, provides multiple opportunities for spiritual development. Any activity within a broad spectrum of experiences can provide for spiritual development when a child is required to directly engage in it and to be aware of the actual moment in which learning is taking place. The religious term 'revelation' is sometimes used to describe those crucial moments when a child suddenly solves a problem or grasps a particular concept and opens the door to new learning possibilities.

An insight into the vastness, intricacies, mystery and the beauty of the natural world can be gained through the science curriculum and can encourage an investigation into the mystery of science itself. Techniques such as role-play allow a child to see the world from the perspective of someone else, to develop their own imagination and develop a sense of empathy. The chance to have fun and to share with others while you learn will also add to a child's spiritual development. Children with severe learning difficulties may require particular support in developing social cognition and in sharing their feelings with others (Hinchcliffe 1994). An approach that improves a child's ability to describe their perceptual experience and depth of feelings will increase spiritual development. Other practices in the school, such as the use of Records of Achievement, children's involvement in the assessment of their own learning, a high regard for metacognition, and placing an emphasis on reward, will have an impact on spiritual development.

Life is not predictable, comfortable and joyful for every child and nor is school. Systems that support children during times of crisis must be in place because children may have to reflect on times of pain and rejection so that they can begin to move forward. Such emotional pain can have a direct effect on a child's potential to learn and may have an effect on their behaviour (Greenhalgh 1994). In order to provide for spiritual development, a school must accept the contingent link between behaviour and learning and develop a concomitant link between the 'academic' and 'pastoral' systems and structures. This is particularly relevant to the secondary sector of education. Academic systems that deal with learning and pastoral systems that deal with behaviour only serve to limit the possibility of providing for spiritual development. 'Teacher in charge of spirituality' is, in reality, an implicit category in every teacher's job specification.

Religious Education and spirituality

RE does have an exceptional role and responsibility in providing for spiritual development in that it deals with the concept of deity and the human response to such a belief. RE is seen as one of the main subject areas through which spiritual development will take place because it can encourage children to consider that something exists that transcends the constraints of the human condition and human experience.

RE can present examples of spirituality as isolated detachment from society as well as devoted duty within society. It identifies paths to spiritual growth through individual meditation and austerity as well as through corporate worship and festivals. It can analyse common human experience and describe the religious response that affects human thought and behaviour. The teaching of RE will promote spiritual development but it can only do so if it is actually seen to be taking place in school.

The RE curriculum enables children to learn from religions as well as about religions in a pluralistic and multi-faith society and therefore the explicit religious content of the subject must not be subsumed into a diluted form of PSE. A school may affirm that it teaches religious education *through* other curriculum areas but it should not claim that it teaches RE *during* other curriculum areas. RE should exist in such a way that the children should identify their learning as taking place in an RE lesson and not believe it to be something else. Although it might include aspects of art, drama, food studies, dance, music or history, RE is a curriculum area in its own right and has something specific to offer. In RE, children can understand and explore how beliefs and values that are associated with religious traditions affect individuals, groups and society as a whole. It should not be an appendage to a topic framework; it should involve the setting of learning objectives that are directly related to outcomes identified in the locally agreed syllabus.

Schemes of work for RE (Brown 1996) should be developed to avoid the knee-jerk response that results in RE being out of context in curriculum planning. An example of this would be the story of Noah and the Ark masquerading as the RE content for a topic on minibeasts. Collective worship will obviously explore themes that have a specific religious content but this is another example of something that must not be dressed up as the area in which all statutory responsibilities for RE are covered.

The 1993 Education Act states that children in special schools will receive religious education 'so far as is practicable' but as with all other children, their parents can request for them to be withdrawn from the subject. The practicability factor is not an issue of ideally available provision and resources; rather it relates to a child's special educational needs. The challenge of providing all children with a differentiated approach to RE, based on the framework of a locally agreed syllabus, is one that teachers and schools must confront. Children who experience learning difficulties may find that RE is a curriculum area where they feel that they can achieve because it does not hold the preconceived fears and anxieties of subjects such as maths or English where they may have experience of limited success. RE and the value it ascribes to diversity and difference can be a subject area that counteracts the marginalisation of such children.

A response to sacred places

The personal response to visiting a place of worship is one example of how the RE curriculum will provide an insight into the spiritual development of individuals and groups. It can indicate whether they can reflect, show empathy or demonstrate respect. An analytical approach to the documentation of comments and responses can provide a framework for assessing spiritual development in relation to the skills, processes and attitudes inherent in an RE curriculum. The following documented comments, from Key Stage 2 pupils in an EBD school, were elicited during a visit to places of worship (O'Brien 1997) and demonstrate a variety of individual responses:

- 'God can be important. I am an atheist but going to a holy place did make me think. It's like a special place, like a forest. A place where nobody can bully you. It made me wonder. I was thinking about many things, but it did not make me believe in God.'

- 'It was so quiet that I started to think. I felt like crying, I don't know why.'

- 'I had to take my shoes off. I didn't want to but you couldn't get in unless you did. We all sat down. I like Ganesha.'

- 'The temple was a bit boring, I knew all about the gods anyway, but the food was good.'

- 'I said a sort of prayer. I said it to myself. At first I made sure nobody was looking. It was a prayer about saying thank you.'

- 'My mum says that the people in the temple are horrible. That's why I said I would spit at them. That's why I was cussing them before we got there. Now I have been inside, I like them. I am proud of what I did.'

Adopting a phenomenological approach to RE expands teaching opportunities and provides access beyond areas of knowledge and understanding to include the broadest range of religious experience. Such an approach of informed empathy would explore the external phenomena of religious belief and practice such as sacred writings and sacred buildings. It will also authenticate the exploration of the individual response to the internal phenomena of religious belief and practice. It can provide a relative cross-cultural framework and context for teaching RE in which the teacher has to suspend their own values. Smart (1997) categorises the dimensions of the sacred as follows – political, economic, ritual or practical, doctrinal or philosophical, mythic or narrative, experiential or emotional, ethical or legal, organisational or social and the material or artistic. An awareness of these dimensions can give an insight into how we can plan to meet spiritual needs through the RE curriculum, remembering that some children may choose to develop a personal relationship with God or with a religious tradition and others may not.

Collective worship

By definition, 'collective worship ' is a time when the school community, or sections of it, gathers together to engage in a personal and communal relationship with God. In our day-to-day language in school we still refer to collective worship as 'assembly' which gives an insight into how it functions for many schools. The concept of worship or deity is not implicit in the use of the word 'assembly', and may point to one of the current difficulties in meeting the legislative requirements.

Circular 1/94 (DfE 1994) guidance states that acts of worship must reflect the broad traditions of Christian belief and in doing so emphasise their Christian character. It also states that acts must reflect an 'appropriate regard to family and faith background, age and aptitude of the pupils'. While this guidance encompasses the range of needs in our schools, it may explain why so many schools feel overwhelmed and uncomfortable about the notion of worship in a diverse educational setting – worship that must be 'wholly or mainly of a broadly Christian character'.

Collective **worth***ship*

Collective worship in an educational setting demands a more rigorous approach to planning. Records should indicate the aim of the act of worship, the level of pupil involvement and an evaluation. Collective worship has to be afforded the same status as other areas of curriculum time.

The term 'worship' has theistic connotations that have been decreed to be broadly of a Christian nature. This is one of the reasons why providing worship in schools presents tremendous challenges and difficulties. When a group of people gather together in a place of worship they arrive with a broad set of agreed beliefs, principles, values and assumptions. They will have a common set of rituals and practices and a commitment to the values that are inherent in a sacred text. They will be travelling together on a religious and spiritual journey defined by the parameters of their faith. They will have attended with the intent to engage with God.

This is evidently not the case in a school. The grouping will not have an agreed set of beliefs and rituals. They will be travelling together on a spiritual journey, which might include a range of paths set out by different faiths. Not all of them will have attended with the intention of praising God. In a multicultural society, schools are composed of a combination of individuals from a variety of the world's major religions as well as others who have beliefs and values that are not related to a concept of deity. The majority of schools are not single-faith communities.

Religious and spiritual experiences should focus on matters of individual, distinct and common *worth*. It is imperative that each school provides acts of collective *worthship*. The time should be spent unpacking the school values, offering pupils time to reflect and respond and presenting them with high expectations of being able to do so. In dealing with issues of worth, the school community will recognise experiences from the range of faith communities that exist within the school. It will investigate themes such as achievement, celebrations and success but must also contain an opportunity to reflect upon matters such as loss, rejection, poverty, loneliness and pain. It must include role-play; opportunities to ask questions and times when active listening might be the main expectation. A variety of demanding and enriching experiences should recognise learning styles so that every child in every school can gain a sense of inner and outer life.

Spiritual restraint

An act of collective worship can be presented as a package that contains a reading, a prayer, time for reflection, and a sacred song. This open and shut package might meet the legal requirement but it is in danger of producing an experience that has little individual meaning for a large proportion of children. The practice of asking children to think about their own god during a time of prayer or reflection attempts to tackle this legislative difficulty. The strict interpretation of the wholly-or-mainly-Christian requirement could entrap many children in a spiritual straitjacket. Special schools, in advocating for the spiritual development of their children, have to guard against the potential for spiritual restraint imposed by the limitations of legislation.

When exploring what is of *worth* to the school community, a school will include themes that are not only broadly Christian but also broadly associated with other faiths and belief systems that strive towards a common good. The common elements of many belief systems is recognised and connections can be drawn between the distinct messages and practices of faith groups. There will also be times when the individual characteristics of a world faith or a belief system can be explored. Effective and interactive collective worship is a time when the school ethos comes alive in an enjoyable physical, sensory, cognitive and emotional experience to recognise and value what is of common, distinct and individual worth to the children, the school and society.

Two spiritual stories

A chapter about spiritual development would not be complete without a story or two! I would like to relate two stories that I have told in special and main-stream schools. They are challenging stories that can be actively experienced through the whole range of senses. They explore themes of a broadly Christian character, although neither is taken from the Christian tradition. I do not intend to describe how the following stories might be told but I would like to assert that access to any story can be increased through a multi-sensory approach. Children build upon their own narrative experience every moment of every day, and participating in story may help them to understand their own experiences. The expressive and symbolic nature of story allows it to be experienced on a variety of levels. I shall highlight some of the main themes and messages as identified by children who have responded to these stories.

King Hiranyakasipu

This story comes from the Hindu sacred writings. It can be found in the seventh canto of the Srimad Bhagavatam. As with many Hindu writings it is always useful to find out the meanings of the names of the main characters before telling the story. This king's name has two parts to it: Hiranya means 'gold' and Kasipu means 'soft bed'. His name gives an accurate insight into his character.

Hiranyakasipu was a powerful and wealthy king who had four sons. He had great wealth but was disturbed by the fact that he would lose it all on the day that he died. His quest for immortality haunted him so much that he decided to take some action. He retired to a remote spot on a mountain and began to meditate. Renouncing worldly trappings, he covered himself in grass and bamboo sticks, sat next to an anthill and began to chant. In the tradition of Hindu ascetics, he meditated for many years and did not eat or drink. The vibrations that spread throughout the world due to his continual meditation began to disturb the animals on the ground and in the air. The rivers and oceans began to churn and the whole surface of the globe began to tremble. The increasing noise reached Brahma, the creator, on a far away planet and he was so concerned that he came to the earth to investigate the source of this disturbance.

Brahma arrived at the mountain and saw an emaciated Hiranyakasipu. He asked him why he was indulging in meditation so powerful that it had caused God to stand before him. The king stated that he wanted a blessing from God in the form of being granted one wish. Brahma agreed to this. In his years of isolation the king had planned this moment meticulously and described his wish to Brahma. 'I do not wish to be killed, I wish to be immortal.' He then proceeded to explain the clauses of his wish. He wanted an assurance that he would not be killed by a human or any of the eight million four hundred thousand species of animal. He did not want to die in the daytime or at night. He did not want to be killed inside or outside of his palace and should not be killed on the ground, in the air and at sea. To cover all eventualities he requested that he should not be killed by any weapon that humankind had invented or would invent.

Brahma agreed to this wish on the condition that the king stopped his meditation. He stopped immediately and was granted his wish. Brahma sprinkled water on the king's head and he miraculously became healthy again. He leapt away from the anthill (where he had become a regular starter on the ants' lunchtime menu) and ran to his palace to celebrate.

He spent his time boasting that he was more powerful than God – after all, he had tricked Brahma into granting him a complex immortality contract. He told people how he had outwitted Brahma and that there was no possible way that he could be killed. He fought armies, convinced that he would not die. He won all of his battles and soon became the most powerful king on earth. He enjoyed his wealth – often to excess. 'He was always drunk on strong smelling wine and his eyes were always rolling.' (Ch. 4, v. 13)

He had a beautiful new palace built. It was made of coral, the walls were made of the most expensive crystal, all of the bedding was made of silk, all seats were bedecked in jewels and it was surrounded by the most fragrant flowers and trees. At this time, one of the king's sons began to anger his father. The child was called Prahlad – which means 'always joyful'. The details of Prahlad's early childhood mark him out as an infinite reservoir of spirituality! He was devoted to God, he helped the poor, he was free from jealousy and arrogance, he was gentle and kind, had many friends and took every opportunity to be kind to animals and plants. Even when his father's servants beat him with sticks he refused to give up his devotion to God.

Prahlad often told his father that he should concentrate on gathering spiritual treasures rather than material ones. Hiranyakasipu did not respond in the most sensitive of ways to this type of advice – particularly from one of his own children. He tried to kill Prahlad by a variety of unsuccessful means. He threw him at the feet of stampeding elephants with no success. He hurled him into a pit of snakes – still no success. He threw him off a hill, exposed him to extremes of weather and tried to stone him to death. Prahlad claimed that God had saved him every time. The king even tried to change Prahlad's views by appointing a private economics teacher to convince Prahlad of the absolute benefits of material wealth. Prahlad, although very young, convinced the teacher that material gain was impermanent and that he should become more concerned with spiritual matters.

One day, the king was walking in his courtyard when Prahlad came to speak with him. The King was expecting him and was already armed with a sword, a shield and a club. Prahlad told the king that the only way Hiranyakasipu's soul could receive liberation from the cycle of reincarnation was for him to give up his wealth and power and to start devoting his life to God. He became very angry and replied 'You speak so much nonsense I shall sever your head from your body. Let me see God protect you.' (Ch. 8, v. 13) Prahlad explained that God had protected him before and would do the same again. Prahlad insisted that God was more powerful than any human would ever be.

The king could not accept this and jumped up and down and in a rage. He clenched his fist and punched one of the pillars in the courtyard. The scripture tells us that 'from the pillar came a fearful sound which appeared to crack the covering around the universe' (Ch. 8, v. 15). Out of the pillar leapt Nrshima – a half-man, half-lion. He was a terrifying sight – 'his nostrils and gaping mouth appeared like the caves of a mountain' (Ch. 8, v. 22). The king attacked him with a club, confident that he could not be killed but Nrshima hurled the king to the ground. Nrshima offered the king a chance to change his ways, but the king remembered Brahma's promise and knew that he could not be killed. He assumed that Nrshima must be scared of him and charged back at Nrshima to continue the battle.

Nrshima was not human nor was he an animal – he was half of each. He was certainly not one of the eight million four hundred thousand species of living things. It was now evening – it was neither day nor night. They were in the courtyard and therefore they were neither inside nor outside the king's palace. Nrshima picked up the king and placed him on his lap – now the king was not on the ground, in the air or on water. Nrshima gripped the king's body with his nails – which were not a weapon made by humankind – and with great strength, tore the king's body apart. Brahma's promise had not been broken.

The gauging of a response from children will allow the teacher to identify the themes and message that the children have received. When I have told this story, the main themes and messages that children have identified include: everybody has to die; God is watching everything; you cannot trick God; even when you pray for something you might not get it; watch out for monsters; if you are kind, God will look after you; do not wish for loads of money – although quite a lot of money is probably OK; sometimes children can know more than adults; don't be greedy; things can happen out of thin air; God is cleverer than kings.

The girl with no name

This Native American Comanche story can be found in the collection *Creation Stories* compiled by Maurice Lynch. I shall highlight some of the themes and messages that children have identified before I relate the story. Children have highlighted: how terrible it feels to be left out of a group; how it is important to remember people who have died; how being brave can be difficult but is important; what it feels like to be taken away from your family; special things that they treasure; how girls can be strong; what it feels like when you are accepted into a group, and whether it is possible to know where God lives. I would prefer to end with the reader responding to it within her or his own individual, distinct and common spiritual context. Adults can respond in the same manner as children by considering, 'How does this story relate to my own story and experience'?

The Comanche people were suffering from a great drought. The land was dusty and cracked and the trees were dying. For weeks the people had prayed their prayer, the dancers had danced it and the drummers had drummed it – but it did not rain. There had been little rain for many years but now it had finally stopped raining. Crops had failed and some of the young and old had started to die. The Comanche were afraid and so they prayed to the Great Spirit. They thought that they must have done something wrong to be suffering in such a way and they asked the Great Spirit to tell them what they had done – but the Great Spirit who lived in the wind did not reply.

A holy man went into the mountains to contact the Great Spirit. He went to the place where there was a burning fire and returned many days later to call the people together. 'The Great Spirit has spoken', he shouted to them. As they gathered he explained that the people had grown selfish. They had taken from the land but they had given nothing back. The greatest sacrifice must be made for rain to fall again. 'We must offer to the Great Spirit the most precious thing that we have in the camp and then life and rain can return to the earth,' he told them.

The people gathered to decide what must be the most precious thing in the camp. The men decided that it must be the tepees that protected their families from frost and hail. The women decided it must be the blankets that they made to keep everyone warm. The young men decided it was the arrows that they made to hunt food. Each thought that they knew which was the most precious thing and so the community talked into the night but they could not reach an agreement.

Whilst the talking took place a girl was sitting by listening. The Comanche people called her 'The girl with no name'. There was a reason for this. All of her family, her parents, her grandparents, her brother and her sister had died in the drought and famine and there was nobody alive to give her a name. She often sat on her own and nobody in the community had asked her for her opinion. She did not feel alone because she always carried a small doll with her. Many years ago her grandfather had brought some wood from the forest. During the winter she watched him carve it until it looked like a human. Her grandmother mixed some dyes from the forest berries and painted the eyes and the lips. Her brother cut some leather with a tool and made a jacket and leggings for it. Her sister found a small bone and polished it so finely that it made a belt. Every morning her father would go into the forest. Sometimes he would return home with the most beautiful deep blue feathers that had fallen from a jaybird. He made them into a head-dress and this was her favourite part of the doll. While the people talked she looked at her doll and she *knew* what was the most precious thing in the community.

When the community had gone to sleep she was left sitting on her own cradling her doll. She was thinking to herself amidst the sound of the birds. She stood up and began to walk into the mountain to 'the place of the fire'. Tears fell down her face as she approached the fire because she knew that this was a moment when she needed to be courageous. As she held her doll over the fire, she remembered all of the people who had helped to create it for her. She knew that if she did not take action now, she never would. Staring into the fire she threw the doll amongst the flames. She stood crying as she saw its outline turn quickly into a gathering of dark ashes. The girl with no name waited for the ashes to become cold and picked them up into her cupped hands. Slowly, she began to throw the ashes to the wind, to the north, south, east and west. The whole experience had made her so distressed that she lay down by the fire and cried herself to sleep.

In the morning the girl with no name was woken by the hot sun blazing into her eyes. She looked around and could not believe what she was seeing. Along the hillside and all over the valley the land was blooming with tiny blue flowers that were quietly rippling in the wind. She knew how this had happened and when the Comanche people saw it they knew too. As she returned to the camp they rushed to greet her and danced around her as they accepted her back into the community. They sang in celebration, and as they did the gentle rain fell from the sky onto the dry earth.

It was on that day that the Comanche people changed her name. From this time she was known as 'the girl who saved her people'. They asked her to name the blue flower on which the rain was now falling, and she did. It still has the same name today – she called it 'Forget me Not'.

Chapter 4

Challenging behaviour: definition, observation and intervention

The description of children as 'disturbed', 'damaged', 'dysfunctional' or 'behaviourally disordered' can result in low expectation of the potential to change behaviour. Such descriptors locate causation within the child and do not encourage the teacher to consider factors such as the quality of the learning environment and the attitude of the teacher. A special school should reject labels that prevent it from being analytical about the contexts of challenging behaviour and creative in designing and implementing interventions. Deficit labels are particularly damaging in the process whereby an image of a pupil is transferred and projected from one colleague to another. Such images are crucial when a teacher becomes an integration advocate.

The labelling of pupils has a direct effect on their integration into mainstream environments (de Wit 1994). The organisation of mainstream integration for children with learning difficulties can be a devastating experience when a teacher encounters the view that difficulties are located and fixed within a child. The experience is made worse when schools are forced to consider the curriculum outcomes of the integration of such children in terms of norm-referenced attainment. A teacher who advocates for a child with learning difficulties has to overcome hurdles such as the effect that the child will have on a school's position in the league table of academic results. This undignified process, where children with learning difficulties become damaged goods, is a harsh reality in a competitive society where learning ability takes preference over learning disability. We must guard against the danger of the concept of 'zero tolerance' being applied to pupils with learning difficulties, thus denying them their rights to integration and inclusion in mainstream settings. A model that supports negative and exclusive thinking will not advance the cause of inclusive and democratic practice.

What is 'challenging' behaviour?

There is a contextual, systemic and social relevance to the term 'challenging behaviour' as well as a meaning that is individual and aetiological. Challenging behaviour could be the result of a child's response to an unstimulating environment, but it may also be another child's response to an environment that is over-stimulating and produces 'sensory bombardment' (Ouvry 1987). A limited range of expressive communication skills might be the cause of behaviour that is judged to be 'challenging'. It cannot be assumed that there will be one factor that determines challenging behaviour – there may be multiple interactive causation that removes the focus away from individualistic explanations.

'Challenging behaviour' has developed into a term that describes behaviour in a variety of educational contexts. I intend to consider the term, and its practical implications, in whatever setting the behaviour takes place. I will also reflect upon the importance of teachers developing the craft of observing behaviour so that they can be in a better position to change it. Observation is a process for gaining data that will help to improve the understanding and quality of teaching and learning in a school.

The importance of a behaviour policy

A school policy should not simply exist as a document that describes what the school believes; it must also describe what a school does. A policy should support the process of implementing whole-school aims and will only do so when it offers clear guidance and provides examples of desired and intended practice. By doing so, it can help to create a positive ethos while simultaneously defining unacceptable practice. A policy is a document that promotes a whole-school approach, and therefore the whole school should be involved in designing and implementing its aims.

A behaviour policy should emphasise the responsibility of all staff and consequently an individual teacher should not be held totally accountable for dealing with challenging behaviour. In difficult situations, a teacher should expect and receive positive support from the school management. The behaviour policy should describe consistent, positive, professional responses as well as articulating how such approaches constitute part of the school's teaching and learning culture. It should indicate the broad aims of the school in relation to behaviour such as asserting a commitment to preventative approaches and defining the rights, responsibilities and expectations of all members of the school community.

It is a small stage of development to describe intention by writing a policy. Real progression will only occur when the policy affects school systems and makes a noticeable and positive contribution to the development of school culture. If the policy is rhetoric for the sake of rhetoric then the documentation will not impact on the daily work of the school.

A benchmark that I use for testing the effectiveness of policies is to consider how the policy would enable a new teacher or a supply teacher to be an effective practitioner. A policy document should give advice to the new teacher on how to implement the school ethos by following recommended and agreed routines and guidelines. The behaviour policy will describe the standards a school aspires towards and the methods it will use to achieve those standards. It will also be explicit about how effective approaches to promoting positive behaviour make a quantifiable difference to the spiritual, moral, social and cultural development of the children.

A supply teacher should not be surprised when, on arrival, she or he is given a précis of the school behaviour policy, an explanation of how an emphasis on reward is implemented in the classroom, and a key name to consult if support is needed due to emerging difficulties. This practice should also be adopted for visitors, so that they can be cued into what is taking place in the classroom and understand the rationale behind it. Supply staff will know that it is not common practice for them to receive such essential information, but a small amount of organisation could make it so. The policy should have such a direct and consistent impact on what takes place in the classroom and around the school that the children cannot afford to have a teacher who is not aware of how to implement it. A policy cannot be allowed to decay on a shelf – it should be alive in practice.

I do not intend to describe the process of designing a whole-school behaviour policy as the reader can explore this in more depth elsewhere (Clarke and Murray 1996). I would like to concentrate on behaviour definition as an aspect of a behaviour policy and to suggest that the responsibility for changing behaviour must be a whole-school issue.

What is challenging behaviour in our school?

A school must have a definition of what it considers to be challenging behaviour in its own context. Consideration of such a definition must occur in an open and honest forum where staff working in the school describe and list actual behaviours that they find 'challenging'. Each person responds to challenging behaviour in individual ways and therefore the list will include a variety of behaviours. Harris *et al.* (1996) conducted a survey of 42 schools for children with severe learning difficulties – from which they received a 75 per cent response. They asked staff to provide an indication of the kinds of behaviours that they found challenging and severely challenging. The list included physical aggression, verbal abuse, smearing, obsessional behaviour, self-stimulation, self-injurious behaviour, running away and resistance to teaching. Isolation and withdrawal did feature on the list but was only judged to be challenging by one school. There are teachers who will read this list and recognise pupils who present a combination of these features. Teachers will also be aware that there will be differences in their school in the manner in which their colleagues are challenged by behaviour.

One colleague may be more challenged by a child that spits than by a child that swears. Another colleague may have developed patient and rational responses to the obsessive behaviours of a particular child. She may then discover that these behaviours, although not outstandingly disruptive, have become so irritating that they have challenged another adult who works with the same child. When describing challenging behaviour, staff should define the outcomes of the behaviours in an attempt to focus on describing what the precise 'challenge' is. A whole-staff description of challenging behaviour is vital in producing a mutually supportive environment where people are not belittled for their feelings about challenging behaviour.

Providing a definition

Emerson (1995) refers to cultural norms and the potential limitation or denial of access to community facilities as factors that must be included in a definition of challenging behaviour. Zarkowska and Clements (1994) describe other component criteria for deciding if behaviour is to be defined as challenging. These include behaviour that is contrary to social norms and behaviour that causes significant stress to those who live and work with the child. The former raises issues about social conformity and normalisation (Wolfensberger 1972) while the latter serves to remind us that children do not stop existing once they leave the school building and that a challenge can be transferred from one context to another. Russell (1997) extends the definition by highlighting the specific challenge that behaviour may present to families.

The use and adaptation of available definitions, such as those mentioned, enables a school to create its own individual school-specific definition of what is challenging. When formulating a school-based definition of challenging behaviour, the following criteria might be considered:

- The behaviour prevents the child from participating in the curriculum. (The school should decide if it wishes to affirm that, in this category, a child who is a persistently passive recipient of the curriculum is as much of a challenge as a child who presents a persistently violent response to the curriculum.)

- The behaviour has a detrimental effect on the learning of other children.

- The behaviour is not considered appropriate to the child's age and level of development.

- The behaviour results in the child being continually isolated from their peers.

- The behaviour has a negative impact upon the child's independence.

- The behaviour is placing extreme threats or demands on individual staff, staff teams or on school resources.

- The behaviour causes the child to be disliked by a significant adult who regularly works with them.

- The behaviour reinforces the child's negative self-concept and low self-esteem.

- The behaviour is restricting the opportunities for a child to develop new skills.

- The behaviour is creating a dangerous environment for the child, for other children or for the adults. This would include self-injurious behaviour.

- The behaviour has a damaging effect on relationships between the school and the person or people who have parental responsibility for the child. This may include the destructive cycle of apportioning blame, where the parent blames the school for the mounting problem or the school blames the parent. Parents offer a chronological and contextual insight into the behaviour of their child, and the school cannot afford to dismiss their expertise.

The purpose of establishing criteria is to ensure that extra support is given to the pupil and the teacher. The criteria should not be manipulated into a checklist through which a child gains cumulative credit points towards exclusion from school. If a teacher feels that a child's behaviour is meeting the criteria defined as 'challenging' in the school behaviour policy, further support should be an expectation not a privilege. This support may include additional resources that enable collaborative solutions to occur. It might also include quality time with a senior manager, or a member of the support services, to reflect on the situation and to design or adapt intervention. The senior manager might offer to teach the class in order to release the class teacher to observe what is taking place.

The process of early identification and acknowledgement of challenging behaviour within the school's defined criteria demands early intervention so that emerging problems can be 'nipped in the bud'. It also gives a fair hearing to colleagues who have a different view of the same behaviour. My 'assertive' child could be your 'aggressive' child and the process of discussing definitions ensures that a colleague's point of view is understood. As with all school policies the ultimate beneficiary must be the child. By defining challenging behaviour we can improve our ability to promote individual and whole-school positive behaviour.

What we say

'She's behaving like this all of the time', 'He's a violent child', 'She's really aggressive', 'He won't behave' or 'He can't behave'. You may have used these phrases yourself and it very likely that you will have heard a colleague use them. They are often used in situations where a teacher is stressed by a child's behaviour and where early intervention has not taken place. I have heard these phrases many times and can think of a young person that I taught many years ago that I used to describe as 'aggressive'. I was describing a small amount of his behaviour, as he could be aggressive, but it had developed into a label that I used to describe him as a person. It was an inaccurate and unjust label. Another inherent danger in the use of such phrases is that they can present a teacher with enough emotional fuel to blame the child for the way in which the child is behaving. The use of such phrases also abandons the clarity that we need when we talk to parents, to colleagues, or to a child, about behaviour and learning.

What it means

It is enlightening to consider how useful each statement is in terms of promoting a change of behaviour. What lies behind the phrase 'She's behaving like this all of the time?' The stress that is caused by minor but regular behaviour difficulties is often contained in such a statement. Of course, it may also be used about high level and threatening incidents. The teacher is feeling unsupported and unable to change an increasingly difficult situation. It is almost certainly a fact that the child will not be presenting challenging behaviour *all* of the time. I do not recommend that the affirmation of this fact be used as a primary response to a colleague who uses this phrase. The phrase may not be accurate in terms of behaviour frequency, but it is communicating a feeling of being persistently overwhelmed and may include an underlying feeling of personal incompetence. The emphasis is on negative behaviour – when you first read this phrase did you honestly think it was a teacher describing a child's positive behaviour?

'He's a violent child' is another statement that implies a child's behaviour has become such a problem that an aspect of the behaviour becomes the descriptor for the whole child. This statement is not contextually precise in relation to where and when he is violent nor does it give any indication that there must be times when he is not violent. It also gives no insight into the positive qualities of the child. He may only be violent for 5 per cent of the time in a school day but this percentage has become enough to focus on his downside – what about the remaining 95 per cent? It is evidently unjust to describe someone based on as little as 5 per cent of her or his behaviour. This statement also gives no indication of frequency and duration of behaviour and thus makes it difficult to design an intervention. The definition of violence would also need to be far more precise in terms of the actions and outcomes of violent behaviour.

Similar concerns apply to the phrase 'She's really aggressive'. There is no clear definition of what the teacher means by aggressive. Does it mean teasing and taunting other children, verbal abuse to children and staff, physical attacks on other children, or is it a combination of some or all of these? Is the teacher's definition in line with school definition? Is the teacher describing a child's actions or making judgements about a personality trait? It would be fair to assume that the use of the word 'really' indicates a degree of severity and frequency that is causing the teacher concern. It may also cause concern for the pupil and their peers too.

In a class containing children with emotional and behavioural difficulties aggression can be used as a powerful tool in the constant struggle to assert hierarchical peer status. One contemporary example that many teachers in EBD schools will recognise is the sentence that begins with 'Your mum . . . .' This is an indicator of inter-peer hostility and an environmental prompt indicating that abuse is about to be exchanged with graded sophistication and degradation. In the unwritten peer culture Code of Practice (Section 1: 'Behaviour'), abuse about your family in general, and your mother in particular, demands a high level response and cannot be ignored.

For those children with significantly developed skills of verbal abuse, 'Your mum' is used as a sentence in itself and there are multiple inferences to be made about the implied abusive meanings. It is a phrase that sets the de-escalation alarm bells ringing in any teacher's head. When a teacher is consistently dealing with such behaviour, and is aiming to reduce and invalidate it, this singular behaviour may be described as aggressive. Although it is by definition 'aggressive', it is also situational and requires an analysis of what might be causing or maintaining it in the classroom.

'He just won't behave' indicates that the teacher has tried to do something but that it has been unsuccessful. 'He just can't behave' indicates a further step along the continuum of hopeless exasperation. It is a statement born out of stress and containing a feeling of exhaustion and lack of competence to effect a change. It gives no indication of the topography of the behaviour; it barely hints at the frequency and implies a focus on negative behaviour. The main difficulty lies within teacher definition of behaviour. Evidently, the child is 'behaving' by breathing and being alive in the classroom, but the behaviour is not what the teacher regards as compliant behaviour within their own terms of reference and values.

Whole-school definitions of desirable and undesirable behaviour are necessary because they demand explicit definition and description of acceptable and unacceptable behaviour and interventions. To obtain clarity when talking about behaviour we must observe and analyse it in relation to improving the quality of learning for the child. Gaining data about behaviour so that the data can inform a change for the better is a craft and competency that teachers should develop. The skills of observation have become more important in a climate where appraisal and inspection place an emphasis on a teacher's ability to self-reflect. Gaining data in order to analyse what the data is telling you is a fundamental skill in the process of changing behaviour. If a teacher is gaining data about behaviour, but doing nothing constructive with it, they should stop collecting it – it is wasting valuable time that could be spent more productively elsewhere.

Why observe behaviour?

We savour moments when new learning takes place whether it is planned or spontaneous. The surge of self-esteem that a child encounters when they experience new learning is a solid foundation for new teaching. Challenging behaviour can limit and reduce these moments and therefore any behaviour that prevents new learning must be seen as a challenge to a learning organisation. If the behaviour is constructing a barrier to learning then we must adopt a rigorous approach to removing the barrier, so that the teacher can focus upon learning need, rather than behaviour difficulty. Systematic observation can support this process.

There are commercially produced schemes for observing behaviour. Authors such as Wragg (1994) describe techniques for the development of context-specific methods of systematic observation in the classroom. The TOAD scheme is a popular observation schedule that is used in the USA and is an example of a scheme that encourages teachers to observe challenging behaviour. Its focus is on Talking out of turn, Out of seat behaviour, Attention seeking and Disruptive behaviour. All of these are negative aspects of behaviour and no emphasis is placed on the positive. Some commercial schemes do not easily transfer to the teacher's point of practice and others may not be compatible with the philosophical stance of an individual teacher. Commercial schemes may require adaptation to reflect the individuality of a school context.

With an increasing emphasis on teachers conducting action research in their own classrooms, observation has to become an important part of our professional practice. Observation challenges us to adopt a stance where we need to obtain detachment from the subjective experiences of reality so that we can ascribe a more specific and detailed meaning to them. When we observe in the classroom, the familiar has to be seen as unfamiliar so that it can become more familiar. Observation empowers teachers to make sure that looking with a critical eye will begin the process of hypothesising. Making integrated connections from observational data can bring about a change in a child's behaviour as well as a change in a teacher's theoretical perspective. The continuous dynamic process of observation will promote change and prevent stagnation in the classroom. Observation raises questions that need to be answered.

For many years the observational skills of behaviour analysis have been in the professional domain of the educational psychologist. I have argued previously that a school should have an eclectic approach to the adoption and integration of pluralistic models and that the psychologist should be a more active source for curriculum development. It is therefore a logical progression that I should assert that the skills of behavioural analysis and intervention design require demystification so that they can become the everyday working tools of every teacher. Psychologists can support this process through professional collaboration thus releasing themselves from the monotonous treadmill of one-off observation sessions producing data for Annual Review meetings. The educational psychologist, who is a trained teacher, should become more involved in supporting learning in the classroom environment. The teacher and the psychologist can be involved in observing behaviour but schools should not forget that, wherever possible, the pupil must be involved too.

What can we observe?

Observation provides us with an insight into the child, the teacher, the learning environment and the intricate and complex interaction between all three. There may be personal factors that affect behaviour. These might include genetic conditions such as Lesch Nyan syndrome, physiological factors such as tiredness, aspects of personality such as a high level of anticipatory anxiety and factors relating to self-esteem such as being unable to see yourself as someone who can learn and achieve.

An observer might consider social factors such as the quality of relationships and the effect of classroom power dynamics on a child's ability to express preferences and make choices. The physical environment is also relevant. Here the observer might consider the amount of planned stimulation and its effect on a child's behaviour. Over-stimulation or under-stimulation can be problematic for all children. For example, individual children with PMLD may prefer to use the natural everyday sounds that exist around them to help them to engage with their environment. Instead, they may be smothered by persistent background music intended to help them to relax.

The psychological environment should also be considered and it is often in this category that teachers have to reflect upon their own behaviour and thought processes. A teacher can consider their expectations for good behaviour, how purposeful the lessons are, and how explicit their teaching and learning intentions are made. We should consider what we say and what we do as our remarks, sometimes said in stressful situations, may trigger or increase a child's challenging behaviour. For example, what function does a remark such as 'act your age' perform when directed at a sixteen-year-old pupil with severe learning difficulties who is presenting challenging behaviour? What effect will it have on their self-esteem? It does not give any indication of what the pupil should do and due to its personal nature there is a high risk of exacerbating the behaviour. It is also a highly offensive comment to make. Analysis of the psychological or emotional environment can be a very effective method for sharing good practice.

The internal and external environment that the pupil experiences, influences, and creates, is complex and organic. Systematic and analytical observation can enable us to make sense of it and to support those vulnerable pupils who find their own behaviour distressing and unfathomable. When observing behaviour, a teacher needs to be clear about the element or combination of elements that they are choosing to analyse. Clarity must exist about those elements that the teacher is choosing to ignore. The teacher must also consider the personal dimensions and agendas that they bring to the observation of children who experience learning difficulties (Bines 1995).

Figure 4.1 indicates four possible elements that we can observe in the classroom where children are presenting challenging behaviour.

Observing nature

Observation can become a valid tool within the school's assessment policy. It forces a teacher to be analytical and reflective about everything they do and

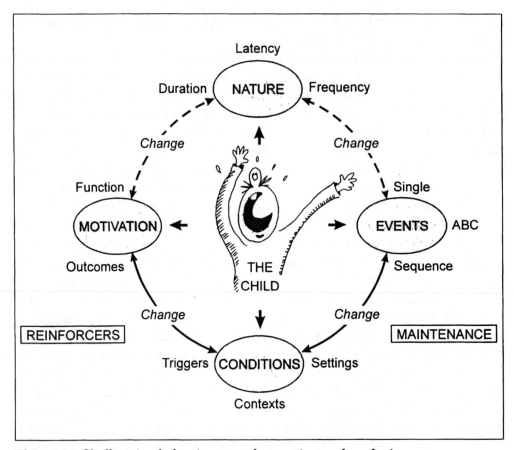

Figure 4.1 Challenging behaviour: an observation and analysis map

how they do it and everything they say and how they say it. Before a teacher decides upon issues of methodology, it is necessary to identify the target behaviour or behaviours for observation and the settings in which they will be observed.

When collecting data about the 'nature' of the behaviour, observations might consider the frequency of the behaviour – how often the behaviour occurs within a specified block of time. This may help to reduce the anxiety of the teacher who feels powerless to change something that is perceived to be happening all of the time. It may also reduce the stress and tension that they bring with them to the observation process itself. Such stress will influence the observational data that is collected and the meanings that the teacher will construct from it.

We may also consider the duration of the behaviour by recording for how long a particular behaviour lasts. If we are serious in our intention to promote a child's positive behaviour then it is vital that we also consider the latency of behaviour. When observing latency, an emphasis is placed on how long it takes before the onset of challenging behaviour. The period of latency gives an indication of positive time as well as challenging time. Observing nature provides information about the topography of a child's behaviour and provides data for the process of behaviour categorisation. Severity or intensity of behaviour may also be considered when observing the nature of a child's behaviour. Herbert (1986) considers the practical methods, and ethical pre-requisites, involved in assessing the severity and intensity of challenging behaviour, from the perspective of a clinical psychologist.

Observing events

A teacher can also observe the situational aspects of behaviour by analysing events. This encourages the teacher not to perceive behaviour as an isolated occurrence but to place it within a sequential context. The observation of this element of behaviour is often associated with the Antecedent-Behaviour-Consequence (ABC) functional analysis model. An observer will consider what happened before the behaviour (Antecedent), describe the observable response (Behaviour) without inferring meaning or motivation, and describe the observable social outcomes and results of the behaviour (Consequence). Con-sequences include 'pay-offs' for the child such as attention or task removal. The ABC approach highlights functional and contingent relationships between the child and the environment. The theoretical framework that underpins this method of observing behaviour is a behavioural one, based on the principles of operant conditioning and generalised reinforcement (Skinner 1953). The behavioural framework has also been applied to the social learning of groups and individuals in schools (Wheldall and Merrett 1984).

Antecedents include those factors and events that act as a prompt for challenging behaviour. In practice, observing antecedents can focus on events that immediately precede challenging behaviour. This might ignore a substantial period of time when a child's behaviour is positive. If this critical time is dismissed, the teacher can fail to analyse the relevant factors that reinforce positive behaviour. When observing events, a teacher has to dif-ferentiate between momentary events or behavioural states and select an appropriate coding system for recording such data (Robson 1993).

Observing conditions

During observation we may want to consider the 'conditions' in which the behaviour occurs. This encourages us to see behaviour within an environmental context and not to simply see it as driven by within-child factors. Zarkowska and Clements (1994) emphasise that each individual must be assessed according to the level of skills that they possess within the environment that is provided for them. The triggers that produce challenging behaviour can be directly related to the conditions in which the child is learning and the coping skills at their disposal.

The roles of each member of staff become increasingly important in a situation where a child presents challenging behaviour. A learning partnership such as that of a teacher and a learning assistant must involve clear communication about the purpose, pace, and role expectation within a lesson. Roles do not come without responsibility and thus the responsibilities for dealing with the possibilities of challenging behaviour must be discussed before a lesson so that inconsistency can be avoided. For example, a teacher may explain that if a child refuses to work and wanders around the room, it will be the teacher who is responsible for intervention. In this situation, the learning assistant can continue working with other children. It may be that the partnership accepts that in a different context, the assistant is the best person to deal with a particular child. A consistent approach may have been agreed for a child who self-injures in the classroom, and both adults will have agreed that the person working with the child at the time will deal with the behaviour. Whatever the situation, the needs of the pupils require effective staff communication.

Relationships are a fundamental aspect of a learning environment and lack of communication can produce a classroom where one adult works while the other waits to be told what to do. It can also produce an environment where, when a difficulty emerges, it receives the undivided attention of every adult in the room. Such a classroom is paradise for a child whose behaviour is geared towards maximum adult attention and an enigmatic riddle for those who have the power to intervene and improve learning, but have not planned to do so.

The 'trigger' for a specific behaviour refers to the stimulus or stimuli that cause it to occur. There may be environmental reasons such as the presence of a particular child or internal triggers such as a child's desire to terminate an activity or to prevent a new activity from taking place. The association between triggers and learned behaviour is not only relevant at the onset of challenging behaviour. The development of trigger phrases or actions that are used during intervention are crucial in achieving goals that are directed at developing child self-control. The relationship between triggers and the nature of the behaviour should be scrutinised, as should the link between the conditions and events in which the behaviour occurs.

Observing motivation

We should also consider the 'motivations' for behaviour – the functions it performs and the tangible or intangible outcomes it provides for the child. Understanding the function of the behaviour from the perspective of the child provides an insight into how the child is making sense of their behaviour within a social context. A functional analysis of challenging behaviour will raise questions about the possible communicative messages inherent in the behaviour (Durand 1990). A common reason given for challenging behaviour is the child's desire for attention – it is proposed that a child might perform 'naughty' behaviour in order to receive attention. This may be the motivational factor, it might be one of the motivational factors, but it is important to accept that there are times when attention is not a motivational factor.

The focus when observing motivation is on the received outcomes for the child – what is in it for the child? A child with learning difficulties may scratch their face and smear blood. They may receive attention from staff to prevent the continuation of the behaviour, but the motivation could be the sensory reward that the experience offers. In this example, the 'pay-off' is self-stimulation not the desire for positive or negative attention.

A child may slap other children and shout and scream when they are asked to attempt a task. This may seem to be another method of gaining attention. Focused observation could produce data that identifies that task withdrawal occurs when the behaviour takes place and this is the pay-off for the child. Task removal is high on the cost-benefit scale for any child with an aversion to work. However, a request to attempt a differentiated task has to be asserted as a reasonable one in a school setting. Attention may be a secondary outcome, but it can still remain a maintenance factor for reinforcing the behaviour. In assessing the motivation for behaviour, a teacher should aim to empathise with the child and see behaviour from the child's perspective without implanting the teacher's own inferences. The focus should be on the child's personal constructs (Kelly 1955) and not on the teacher's. Many observation and intervention schemes place an emphasis on observable behaviour to prevent this from happening.

Through observation we must gain an insight into our potential to change behaviour by considering the issue of alterability of need. When we have deconstructed and analysed data, we can begin to investigate which components are functioning as maintenance factors – factors that keep the behaviour going and cause it to re-emerge. This enables the teacher to return to the context and to observe again. Extrinsic or intrinsic maintenance factors will have a direct influence on the nature and topography of the behaviour. Changing the relevant environmental and internal influences places an emphasis on a teacher's ability to alter maintenance factors and to ultimately change behaviour.

The change to positive behaviour may occur rapidly or over a longer period of time. Many teachers will have experienced the realities of the phrase 'It will get worse before it gets better', when new interventions appear to increase the frequency and intensity of challenging behaviour. Intervention should be planned over a time schedule relative to the individual child and the level of the behaviour in question so that long-term progress is not hindered by short-term problems.

Through observation and analysis of the four main elements illustrated in Figure 4.1 we can establish a holistic behaviour map for a child. This enables a teacher to design intervention. I would like to assert that even the most minimal intervention could be construed as an intrusion into a child's life and right to self-determination. Even when it is morally and ethically defensible to intervene, such as in the case of severe self-injurious behaviour, we should remain cognisant that an intervention, no matter how significant we judge it to be, may be unwanted by the child.

Intervention – initial issues

The debate about aversive and non-aversive intervention has to be seen in relation to the interface between the legislative and school context. When defining and describing challenging behaviour, the staff should also define and describe what constitutes non-aversive and aversive intervention: what is acceptable and what is unacceptable. I would suggest that minimally invasive and intrusive interventions should be the basis for designing respectful intervention. The Children Act (1989) states that the deprivation of food is illegal – but can we safely claim that it does not exist as a threatened or actual punishment in every school? This example highlights the necessity for the rigorous monitoring of intervention to prevent a situation where agreed whole-school interventions are blatantly undermined behind the closed doors of the classroom without accountability to the child, the school or the parents.

Physical restraint

The use of physical restraint must be the final option, take place within the legal framework, and respect human dignity. Physical restraint can be used to prevent a child from significantly harming her- or himself, significantly harming others, or from causing serious damage to property (DfE 1994). The Department of Health guidelines (1993) make a distinction between 'holding' and 'restraint'. This is determined by the degree of force being applied, and the intention to discourage or to prevent a child from causing self harm, harm to others, or damage to property (Farrell 1995). It should involve minimal reasonable force and should seek to avoid injury (Hewett and Arnett 1996). Staff will make an on-the-spot professional judgement about 'significance' and 'seriousness' and this must be informed by clear policy guidelines. Each individual interpretation should provide intervention that is within the boundaries of institutionally agreed modes of good practice. Evaluation of school physical restraint policy and practice requires external monitoring so that practices such as the notorious 'pin-down' method are not allowed to take place.

Physical restraint is not a punishment nor is it acceptable as a punishment. When it has to occur, the child should be told why it has to happen, and talked to calmly during it. Staff should judge the earliest moment at which the restraint can stop, so that self-control can be handed back to the child. Every incident must be recorded and parents should be informed that it has taken place (Lyon 1994). There is a temporary loss of dignity to all parties involved when physical force becomes the last action in an attempt to resolve a difficulty – even when all other preventative skills aimed at terminating the behaviour have been exhausted and there is not an autocratic intention behind it.

The ethos of the school will be determined by the visible link between desirable and actual methods of intervention. Schools should remain aware that an ethos shift is always a possible outcome when selecting and employing intervention. Decisions relating to intervention should be taken within the gender and socio-cultural context of each individual, as well as their distinct and individual learning contexts. Physical intervention is not the only restraint method where moral and ethical issues and principles have to be discussed by staff and parents. Pharmacological interventions can have restraint as their main purpose and in these situations the development of the whole child has to be considered. The use of interventions that result in the chemical containment of children can produce a regime of passivity that is disrespectful to children and limits their personal development (O'Brien 1996).

Differential approaches

In every school, there should be professional debate about how to reduce challenging behaviour by promoting positive behaviour. This is not a bland and vacuous cliché; it is a practical and coherent whole-school philosophy and approach. The sensitive use of specific differential interventions (Clements 1987) can promote positive behaviour and the interventions and outcomes should always be ethically defensible.

A differential approach will focus on promoting positive behaviour in an attempt to reduce and eliminate challenging behaviour. An example might be the case of a child who experiences learning difficulties and swears. In an attempt to reduce and extinguish the swearing, the teacher will catch the child when they are not swearing and remark about how positive that is. This systematic reinforcement of positive behaviour is referred to as differential reinforcement of other behaviours (DRO). It aims to reinforce the absence of challenging behaviour. A differential approach could also be used to acknowledge the reduction of swearing to a certain frequency or limit. The initial challenging behaviour is being reduced and the child receives positive reinforcement for making a graded change in their behaviour. This is referred to as differential reinforcement of low rates of behaviour (DRL). Differential reinforcement might be targeted at a behaviour that is incompatible with the challenging behaviour – for example a child that self-injures through biting might receive positive reinforcement for behaviours that make biting physically impossible.

Consideration of the potential use of functional equivalence is a vital component in the process of promoting positive behaviour. Once the motivation for a child's challenging behaviour has been assessed and confirmed, other behaviours can be taught or selected that perform the same function as the challenging behaviour – these new behaviours are functionally equivalent. A child may disturb the learning of other children in order to gain teacher attention. The teacher can intervene and teach new acceptable behaviours which perform the same function for the child. The implicit and explicit message is that the child does not need to be challenging to demand teacher attention because the teacher has taught the child which behaviours will gain attention. The teacher has to ensure that those behaviours are recognised, reinforced and rewarded. The ultimate aim of differential methods is for positive behaviour to crowd out negative behaviour.

For some children, there is a need to teach discriminatory skills that are functionally equivalent. This might involve teaching pupils who experience learning difficulties a more acceptable method of communicating and asserting their entitlement to say 'no' as well as 'yes'. This is a more important step towards autonomy than what can become an obsessive special school emphasis on learning to say 'please' and 'thank you'. Skills that establish autonomy are also relevant for adults with learning difficulties who can become entrapped in an oppressive and submissive model of lifelong learning within a framework that they have not helped to construct. For those children that have a fear of failure, the use of techniques such as errorless discrimination learning (Wishart 1991), can help them to feel a sense of success at the start of a task before it increases in complexity and demand.

Observation as surveillance

Observation is an analytical process that contains many ethical and moral issues (Hitchcock and Hughes 1994). An effective approach to observation will have its parameters set by the subjective experience of the child. To begin to have an informed opinion about a child's subjective constructs will require varying degrees and methods of observation. There is an ethical necessity to respect a child's sensitivity to being over-observed and to respect their right to individual privacy.

A pupil from an EBD school spoke to me about an integration experience at a local middle school: 'I had forgotten what it was like. To be honest I did have a small fight in the playground. The thing was though, it was so big at that school that nobody found out, and I didn't get into trouble like I would here.' This may appear to have little to do with developing an observation schedule but it actually highlights the fact that a special school is often a small place where there is nowhere to hide. Children with SLD or PMLD may experience an environment where multi-professional observation and assessment is almost a daily curriculum experience. We must not underestimate the emotional impact that over-observation can have. The special school should not be a surveillance society. Conscious efforts should be made to provide a broad, balanced, relevant and differentiated approach towards observation for each individual.

Think before you intervene

The term 'challenging behaviour' implies that someone somewhere will be challenged by it. The teacher can apply techniques that reduce the challenge and develop a mental model that will improve the likelihood of successful intervention and outcomes. When talking about the political difficulties in Ireland, Disraeli commented, 'The moment you think you have found the answer to the Irish question, the Irish change the question.' We could adapt this saying and propose that the moment you think you are being challenged by a child's behaviour – try to change the challenge. In the split seconds of intervention, the adult should undergo the process of re-describing or re-framing the challenge in a calm and rational fashion. This may happen through their internal voice reminding them to model calmness and respect, or it might be articulated to the child in few precise words explaining the behaviour that the teacher wants. Once in self-control the teacher can begin the process of removing the challenge completely.

The process of internal visualisation and positive mental rehearsal provides a focus on a mutually desired outcome. This can enable the desired outcome to occur. It can also prevent the teacher from being distracted by behaviours that take place during intervention. Imagine a potentially threatening and violent situation where a child has trashed a room, peers have been removed so that there is not an audience for the behaviour, but the child continues making threats. In this situation, a reality in special schools, a teacher who is intervening can visualise the child in a calmer state and the room being returned to its original condition. This may seem an impossibility at the entry point of intervention, and the child may behave in a way that seems to undermine such an eventuality, but in a school with a structured and sensitive approach to intervention this outcome will happen. The teacher remains in control and does not intervene with body language that can imply a competition for aggressive supremacy.

In visualising such an outcome the teacher can recontextualise the behaviour, focus on resolution, and offer a 'way out' for the child. Ultimately, the child can begin to understand the process and product of their behaviour and develop skills that enable them to change. For many children this will involve the teaching of new communication skills, developing a new repertoire of social skills, and where possible the introduction of self-reflection. As soon as there are signs that behaviour is changing for the better, the child must receive recognition and praise for implementing the change from those who have helped to mediate it.

Self-esteem

Personal involvement in a change, no matter how many others have been part of the process of the mediation of that change, will result in an increased sense of autonomy and an improvement in self-esteem. Adults can support the change in behaviour but it is the child that actually makes it happen. With this in mind, it is important that interventions have some degree of implicit success built into them, and that they are carefully monitored and evaluated to prevent the lack of autonomy from becoming contagious. Without some guarantee of success, the pupil and the teacher can become de-skilled, both feel less competent, mutual trust can be damaged, both question their potential for self-determination and the temperature of the self-esteem thermometer plummets.

Chapter 5

Battle zone or learning zone?
Classroom strategies

Nior bhris focal maith fiacal riamh
A kind word never broke any teeth
(Irish saying)

Strategies for promoting positive behaviour will be most effective when the school's aims are clear, there is conceptual clarity about learning need, there is an explicit link between behaviour and learning, and interactions are based on respect. The approaches and strategies outlined in this chapter will apply in special and mainstream schools. Each strategy will have a different application and meaning to the individual context in which a child is being taught. Some teachers may feel that there are strategies that do not apply to their particular situation. However, the teacher should recognise the connections between the strategies and select those that work best for them in their classroom. The approaches are based on respectful, positive and responsive relationships and are combined with sensitive, flexible and needs-driven strategies.

I accept that some colleagues, perhaps those who are embarking on a new career in teaching in mainstream or special education, may have opened the book at this chapter with their 'tips for teachers' antennae anxiously twitching. I urge them to read the preceding chapters, so that the practical approaches and strategies for promoting positive behaviour can be understood in the connective context of a coherent and theoretical learning framework.

When adopting and implementing strategies, a teacher should critically reflect upon their own practice. A starting point would be to ask yourself – does the way that I understand, analyse, prevent and intervene during challenging behaviour place me in the 'battle zone' or 'learning zone'? The characteristics of both zones will become evident, but I shall describe some elements in order to provide an initial overview. A teacher in the learning zone will see a child's *behaviour* as a challenge whereas a teacher in the battle zone will see the *child* as the challenge. In the battle zone there are barriers between the teacher and the pupil – in the learning zone bridges replace those barriers. In the battle zone teaching styles can be oppressive and manipulative but in the learning zone they are responsive. It is my contention that a teacher in the learning zone has more power to raise the standard of teaching and learning and can offer more opportunities for mutual spiritual, moral, social and cultural development. To enter the learning zone the teacher must be willing to reflect upon their own behaviour and have a fundamental commitment to the belief that environments and people can change.

'Inspirated to learn'

The professional skills and personal qualities of a teacher determine their position in either zone. Barber (1996) produces a summary list of the desired positive skills and qualities of a teacher. The personal qualities include: a good understanding of self, a generosity of spirit, a sense of humour, a concern for others, intellectual curiosity and a willingness to undertake professional training. The skills include an understanding of the curriculum, understanding how children learn, and an ability to plan appropriate learning programmes.

In a series of semi-structured interviews, I discussed the question of 'what makes a good teacher?' with pupils who attended EBD schools. Many of them had been placed in special schools since the early years of their school career. This is not a broad representative sample and I make no claim for the wider validity of what they have to say. A more comprehensive approach to gaining pupils' perspectives is available (Garner and de Pear 1996; Lloyd-Smith and Davies 1995).

The pupils spoke about their perception of a good teacher. This was someone who understood their emotional and behavioural learning difficulties and helped them to make progress in their learning. The list is presented in their language, with their explanations. It aims to provide valid illustrative material for the purpose of raising issues. Their strength of feeling about this matter was evident in their constant use of expletives, which were removed when compiling this list:

- Strict – They like you but they do not let you do what you like.

- Well organised – They have thought about the lesson and they don't say, 'What shall we do now?' halfway through it.

- Understanding – They give you work that makes you feel better inside. They just know how to do it.

- Their words – Sometimes they say something that makes you feel better like 'We all make mistakes, but look at all of the good work you have done.' They don't give you bad chat like 'You can't do nothing. You are stupid for someone of your age.'

- Not rude – They don't put you down and they don't shame you up when you ask for help. Good teachers know that sometimes it is not your fault if you don't understand the work.

- Fun – They make the lessons interesting so that you understand it.

- Respect – They treat you like the age you are.

- High standards – As one pupil stated 'Even if you are thick, a good teacher will make you do the best you can so you have your own high standards. You know if the work you do is crap – like you haven't tried hard, it's nowhere near your best, or you couldn't care – and a good teacher will not let you get away with doing crap work. If you get away with crap work then you know that you go to a crap school.'

- Good attitude – If the teacher's attitude to you is good then your attitude to the work is good. They don't make you copy loads of work out just to keep you quiet – that winds you up, it doesn't make you quiet.

- 'Inspirating' – School can be a waste of your time. If you get sent to a special school for behaviour problems your mates say it's a school for 'nutters' or 'mental cases'. You should get work that helps you with life. A good teacher will inspirate you to learn!

These pupils are examples of the kind that Cooper (1996) presents as markers for those aspects of the school environment that are socially and personally 'toxic'. They are the pupils who react more swiftly and more overtly to negative experience than the majority of their mainstream peers. The implementation or avoidance of certain teaching styles and interactions will enable a teacher to promote positive behaviour and remain in the learning zone. Learning that you can learn, learning how to learn and being inspired to learn will keep pupils in the learning zone too.

Positive prevention

There are certain preventative approaches that can be adopted when teaching pupils who experience learning and behaviour difficulties. However, there are certain inter-teacher behaviours that can prevent colleagues from experimenting with new approaches and from making progress. I have a moral responsibility to mention one of them.

Ban 'He's all right with me!'

I do not need to set the scene, as it could be any classroom in any school across the country. A teacher is finding a particular pupil difficult – the choice of gender in the heading is deliberate, as it is most likely that the pupil will be a boy. The teacher has tried everything but still the child's behaviour deteriorates, disturbs others and distresses the teacher. Arriving in the staff room in need of a serious caffeine injection, the teacher decides to share his worries with a colleague and explains that he has a difficulty with a particular child.

This act of professional bravery is done in the hope that empathy or advice will ensue. The response given is the verbal equivalent of a swift kick in the groin: 'He's all right with me.' I have heard this phrase many times and witnessed the desperate response of a colleague on the receiving end of it. It is a phrase that can be adapted for whole classes too: 'They're all right with me.' It would be interesting to see the results of research into the absolute truth and reliability of this statement in relation to those teachers who use it. The Minister for Education should be given the legislative power to take immediate action and ban the singular and plural versions of this morale-wrecking phrase from our schools.

Share the management of behaviour

The implied power balance within the phrase 'behaviour management' is not especially helpful when planning to change a child's behaviour. This power relationship can be manipulated or interpreted so that the teacher possesses all of the management power. A teacher may decide that a child has a behaviour difficulty that requires behaviour management or modification. The teacher takes the decision to 'sort out' the behaviour for the child. In this context the locus of control is always the teacher. In order to promote positive behaviour, the teacher must be willing to share power and accept that the child has a significant and ultimately vital role to play in altering their behaviour. A dominance–subordination paradigm of behaviour management is not the most effective or respectful method of changing behaviour, even if it is shown to work in some situations.

The teacher who decides to manage a child's behaviour without involving the child is adopting a strategy that belongs in the battle zone. Such an intention can produce confrontational interactions that are driven and dominated by status. Continual use of these strategies can categorise the child as the enemy within. When a teacher acts and behaves as if their personhood is determined by their status they will encounter difficulties with children who reject such status. Approaches that are based on respect rather than status are essential when working with every child. They are particularly important for those children who are puzzled by the concept of status, as some children with severe learning difficulties might be. I am not stating that a teacher should not be in charge of setting consistent boundaries, I am highlighting the difference between assertive authority and oppressive control.

Challenging situations will occur in any classroom where there are children who are emotionally fragile and who experience learning difficulties. These children may have a 'knock on' effect and influence the behaviour of others. In such situations, a teacher may have concerns beyond individual children that develop into anxieties about the general behaviour of the class. Such staff will find the 'exposition of teaching skills for classroom management' (McManus 1995) a comprehensive list that will apply to most mainstream environments. They will also find the work of Rogers (1991) particularly helpful in creating a positive climate in a mainstream classroom.

Avoidance techniques

Those pupils who were interviewed identified the attitude of the teacher as an important factor in promoting a positive relationship. Hargreaves *et al.* (1975) present a polarised categorisation of teachers who are 'deviance-insulative' and 'deviance-provocative'. This polarisation does not seem to acknowledge the complex psychosocial interactions that contribute to the perpetually changing balance of teacher attitude. Pupils receive and interpret a teacher's attitude through the ways that teachers speak and behave towards them as groups and individuals. So what can teachers do to develop a mutually responsive relationship that prevents negative pupil behaviour and promotes positive behaviour? They can begin by adopting their own avoidance techniques.

Avoid sarcasm

Sarcasm is based on the hierarchical abuse of power. A teacher–pupil relationship should not have a pupil's fear of public and personal humiliation as its foundation. In practical terms, a sarcastic approach can result in angry responses from pupils and an incremental build up of furious resentment. A teacher who uses scathing public put-downs and personal comments as a system of control is likely to win the battle in a war of words against weaker opposition. The battle may be won but the respect of the pupils is lost. There is a great difference between sarcasm and humour. Humour can often take unnecessary tension out of a situation and will never be directed at a person in order to humiliate them. Respectful humour is a feature of the learning zone. Sarcasm is the corrosive sediment of the battle zone.

Avoid personalising a child's behaviour

A classroom is a demanding place and a teacher will invest vast quantities of time and effort into creating her or his individual version of the least restrictive learning environment. A classroom often becomes a reflection of the teacher's personality, and in this context it is not surprising that a teacher may interpret a child's challenging behaviour in a personal way. Some teachers will become disillusioned when they meet pupils who refuse to understand that the teacher has stayed awake until the early hours of the morning preparing work for them. Painstaking preparation can be destroyed in a few moments by the aggressive, dismissive or disruptive response of a child.

When a teacher works with a child who presents challenging behaviour, the teacher may ask, 'Why is this child doing this to *me*?' The teacher may feel that there appears to be no particular reason for the challenging behaviour. It is important to collect observational data when a behaviour feels as if it is personal so that the teacher can become analytical about causation. Otherwise, behaviour that appears to have no reason will be construed as behaviour that is personally directed. The stress of such a situation also changes the teacher's focus from the behaviour to the child. This presents the danger of such a predicament developing into a personality clash. A personal interpretation may also prevent the teacher from understanding the functional messages of the behaviour from the child's perspective. A child with SLD may continually pull a teacher's hair as a means of exploring its texture. This may be because they use sensory experiences to help them to make sense of their world. A child who has been sexually abused may physically attack a teacher because they confuse positive and negative relationships and resent what adults represent to them. In both cases the teacher *receives* the behaviour but is not the *cause* of the behaviour – it is not personal.

Unfortunately, it is a fact that there might be occasions when a child's behaviour is a consequence of a negative interaction initiated by a teacher. In this situation, it is the teacher's responsibility to de-personalise such behaviour, reflect upon the quality of their relationship with the child and to make a conscious effort to be positive.

Avoid making threats or promises that you cannot keep

The threat that is not carried out will undermine a teacher's authority. In times of stress, teachers must avoid using serious and severe threats that they will be unable to implement unless they receive the full support of the emergency services and the armed forces. The regular use of smaller scale threats that are not followed up is also an ineffective method of asserting authority because children soon learn the rules of this game.

It is important that a threat is perceived as a sanction – something that the pupil understands to be part of the school system and not a personal attack upon them. It is vital that they know that there are staff who will ensure that contingent and appropriate consequences will follow unacceptable behaviour. Rogers (1991) illustrates that it is the certainty of consequences, rather than their severity, which will have a direct effect on the disruptive behaviour of a pupil.

When a pupil is making threats, even if their behaviour history suggests they do not carry them out, it is always advisable to take the threat seriously. A teacher should never create a situation where their intervention is perceived as inviting a child to carry out a threat because of what the teacher has said or done during intervention. Dismissing or demeaning a child's threat will increase the likelihood of the threat being performed.

The consistency and organisation required in ensuring that sanctions take place must be applied to the positive side of teaching. If a teacher makes a promise to a child they should follow that up too because a promise made by a teacher informs the pupil that she or he is significant and valued. The broken promise will have a devastating effect on the self-esteem of the pupil and will damage their relationship with the teacher.

Avoid loaded language

Loaded language is evident when we speak to children and about children. When commenting on children's work, teachers should avoid the phrase: 'I like it *but*...' The pupil will interpret this as a statement meaning that the teacher does not like the work at all, and it will be received as criticism. If a teacher likes a pupil's work they should say what they like about it. At a later time they can offer advice or enquire about areas that might need improving or extending by saying 'Tell me about . . .' or asking 'Have you thought about . . .?' or 'What do you think about . . .?' Depositing these positive nuggets into conversations with pupils is better that employing a phrase that will be received as language loaded with criticism.

It is always important to be aware of the way in which we describe children – particularly those children who experience learning difficulties or who are physically disabled. Descriptive terms can be loaded with assumptions, values and expectations. I once taught a pupil who said 'I want the teachers to judge me on my abilities, not on my disabilities, because my abilities far outweigh the others.' This is excellent advice for any teacher. If we see the disability first, then we may never see the individual. Lewis (1995) cites a reported example of a woman who was blind, asking for directions in the street. She felt that the person that she had spoken to was ignoring her. The passer-by explained why the woman had not heard the directions – they had been given to her guide dog. We have to be aware of the type of language that we use so that we can respect the individual needs of children and see and talk beyond the disability or difficulty.

Some of the most well-meaning colleagues still casually describe pupils who are non-ambulant as 'the chairs' or 'wheelchairs'. We have to consider the implications of such labels for our expectations for the pupils in the variety of contexts in which they encounter us. The common practice of describing secondary-age pupils with severe or profound and multiple learning difficulties as 'developmentally young' can also affect expectation. Although unintended, this phrase does create a visual image of adolescent babies.

Positive approaches

The learning zone offers many approaches that will transmit a positive attitude and develop positive relationships. Preventative steps can prepare the way for developing the type of relationships that will remain intact after an incident where challenging behaviour has occurred.

Contact parents to report positive achievements

Parents will know from the school calendar that there will be planned times, such as annual parents' meetings, when they are expected to have face to face contact with the teacher. The experience of the parents whose child presents behaviour difficulties is that a school is more likely to contact them during times of crisis or concern. A school should develop structures that ensure parental contact is a planned response to the positive achievements of an individual child.

I received an insight into a specific parental perspective during the introduction of a school achievement week. The children were informed that three pieces of good work would entitle them to make a phone call to their parents. An adult would support the phone call if the child requested this. The first child came to make his call. He had completed his third piece of good work and his reward was immediate. It was vital to stop everything and capture the moment, because five minutes later things may not be have been going so well for him. He asked me to ring his home to inform his mother that he was standing by the phone waiting to say something. His mother answered, heard my voice, and asked, 'What has he done now?' I handed the phone to the boy who replied 'Good work Mum!' She insisted that I spoke to her again and apologised for her response. Her explanation was that she had been conditioned by a history of schools that had been unable to contain her son. Her perception was that they had constantly phoned her to complain or to request her immediate attendance to collect him. She felt that the schools were blaming her for his difficulties. The phone call had made her pleased with her son and with the school. He was busy telling adults and children that he had been good and he talked of getting a treat when he got home. Positive feedback to parents goes a long way.

Respect and acknowledge gender, race and culture

The common, distinct and individual needs of children are inextricably linked with their gender, race and culture. A teacher should ensure that there is a balanced ratio of attention between boys and girls, particularly during lessons where talk is the main tool for learning. Positive images of both genders should appear in resources and activities. Schools should also be aware of gender issues when examining procedures for intervening during disruptive behaviour. If men dominate the hierarchical structure of the school, there should be a conscious effort to ensure that control is not based on stereotyped male characteristics. Power should be shared out in an attempt to prevent the creation of a 'wait till your father gets home' culture of discipline.

If we are to meet the needs of the whole child then we must acknowledge and value their race and cultural background. A statement such as 'I do not notice their race or colour; they are all children to me' promotes an approach that can only meet the common needs of an amorphous mass of children. It does not recognise or value individual difference and diversity. Someone's race and culture is part of their individual identity as a member of a cultural community. It is something that is important to them and is deserving of respect. They should not be the victims of institutional colour-blindness.

Teachers should talk to pupils about their culture but remain sensitive to the fact that just because a child comes from a specific cultural or faith community, it does not make them an expert on the history and practices of that community. The importance of understanding culture and race is crucial in promoting a relationship where pupils feel that what they contribute as a person is valued by the teacher.

I am reminded of an incident that speaks for itself and belongs in the 'unbelievable but true' collection of teaching anecdotes. One afternoon, in a mainstream school, a subject teacher rushed a Year 10 pupil into my office. He had been given a pristine folder in which to keep his work, a folder that had been paid for out of the departmental budget. The class had been instructed to write their names on the folder, but this boy had written 'Malcolm X' in bold black letters instead. The boy, born in London of African-Caribbean parents, did not predict how the teacher would respond to an act that was perceived as defiant and non-compliant behaviour. The teacher brought him to the office constantly enquiring 'Is this your name?' After a period of intervention, the boy answered this plainly ridiculous question and admitted that it was not his name. He also apologised and offered to buy a new folder. The difficulty was resolved within the terms that the subject teacher had insisted upon. When the boy had left the office, my colleague pointed to the folder on which 'Malcolm X' was emblazoned and said to me, 'Anyway, who is this Malcolm the Tenth?'

Strive to demonstrate fairness

When a teacher adopts a respectful model of teaching they will always try to be fair. This involves the sharing of attention and the equitable distribution of justice. A teacher should show that they do not have any favourites through their positive interaction with every child. This is far more desirable than the children believing that their teacher has no favourites because they actually dislike every pupil.

Colleagues who teach in an EBD school will know that the crusade for equitable individual and group justice is championed daily, with vigour, by many of their pupils. It is a particular skill to be able to negotiate with pupils who believe that everything must be done according to their own agenda. Such pupils have to learn that this cannot be the case in a school. There is not an inherent weakness in being fair, as pupils understand that a fair teacher is also a firm teacher. In demonstrating fairness there will be times when a teacher has to apologise. A teacher might single out a 'culprit' and when the bigger picture becomes clear, realise that their perception of what took place was not completely accurate. In these situations an apology to the child is a sign of strength rather than weakness. It will demonstrate that a teacher is fair and will place the teacher in a positive position for future interactions with the pupil. It also places the teacher and the pupil in the learning zone.

In creating a learning environment that is fair to all, the teacher must be supported by a flexible school framework for rules, rewards and sanctions. As Nolan (1987) urges, 'bend the rules to match the need'. The implementation of distributive justice should follow the principles of the differentiated curriculum – each person should be considered according to their individual needs. In this respect, being fair really does mean treating everyone differently.

Seek support

A teacher should not be expected to work in isolation. It is likely that every teacher will need support from their colleagues at some point in their career. Teamwork promotes effective working practices and collaborative relationships involve a consistent commitment to supporting each other. Support should be available at times of creativity as well as times of crisis. There are always teachers who are willing to give their goodwill and support to a colleague who is finding an experience challenging. Schools should institutionalise systems of collegial support so that they operate on grounds of professional responsibility as well as upon goodwill.

A teacher should seek and expect support during difficult times; it should not be seen as something that is unusual or an imposition on the time of other colleagues, particularly those in a management position. A teacher should not be forced into a situation where they breathe a sigh of relief when they hear that a child who is presenting challenging behaviour is absent from school. If the teacher is at a point where, upon hearing such news, they secretly wish that the child had flu (which will prolong the absence), then it is an indicator that support needs to be sought. If the teacher has a nocturnal version of irritable child syndrome – where a particular child presents challenging behaviour in a teacher's dreams as well as during the school day – then support is required immediately. Teaching does not have to be that stressful.

Providing opportunities for teachers to observe and learn from each other is a feature of the learning zone because it formalises the process of the sharing of skills. One salutary reminder: a newly qualified teacher should not judge who they can learn from solely on the basis of the years of teaching experience that a colleague has behind them. Some colleagues who have been teaching for years will have continued to learn as each year progresses. They will be outstanding examples of how to provide high quality teaching. Others may have years of experience that amounts to one year repeated over and over again. Twenty years' teaching experience does not necessarily equate to twenty years of learning.

Use positive class rules

The school behaviour policy must affect, and be affected by, what takes place in the classroom. Class rules can be an effective adaptation and reminder of school rules as well as an explicit statement of the standards that an individual teacher expects. If possible, the pupils should be involved in the discussion and negotiation of rules. This has to be done in an honest fashion because pupils have to understand that some rules are available for explanation and illustration, not negotiation. The school and the class teacher own the professional responsibility to set clear boundaries for the pupils.

One benefit of discussing rules with pupils is that they can be written in words that the children use and identify with. They should also be written in positive terms – what the pupils *should* do. The best classroom rules will give an explicit indication of the type of person that a child should aim to be – they offer an insight into spiritual and moral development. The teacher should aim to offer positive praise to the children for keeping to the rules rather than waiting until they are broken and using them as punitive punctuation points in a lesson.

In issues where potential confrontation exists, the teacher can remove the personal element of confrontation by stating that the pupil agreed to a specific rule being employed in the classroom. If this rule reinforces a whole-school rule, then the argument about the rule is between the pupil and the school, not between the pupil and the teacher.

I would recommend that class rules have a ceiling of five or six because beyond that it is difficult for children to remember the rules and put them into practice. It is worth remaining aware that many adults cannot remember the Ten Commandments. Sizeable proportions of those who can remember them have difficulty implementing them. It is more common for these 'golden rules' of the Judaeo-Christian tradition to be interpreted as if they were questions on a GCSE examination paper: select three commandments from ten, attempt them to the best of your ability, and remember to refer to your coursework. When setting and negotiating rules, always aim to avoid inventory overload.

Use rewards

Rewards should recognise achievement and progress as well as attainment. They can also be extremely effective in reinforcing desired behaviours. A functional analysis of a child's challenging behaviour will give a teacher insight into the reward that maintains and reinforces the behaviour. Rewards should be used in line with a child's individual needs – for some children deferred reward is a concept that does not match their stage of development. In such cases rewards must be meaningful, age-appropriate and immediate. Rewards systems can operate on a whole-school, class, or individual pupil level. Individual methods are powerful currency for a child who has low self-esteem, a fragmented sense of belonging, and who needs targets that are achievable and challenging.

When setting individual targets relating to behaviour and learning for younger children, it is often best to display their achievement and progress in a large and bright visual format. One of my colleagues used an individual race-track for this purpose. Three children had been set specific targets and three large individual race-tracks were made. It was not a race circuit where the children competed against each other. Each child's photo was placed on a car to give the impression that they were driving it. Each individual set off knowing that evidence of an agreed unacceptable behaviour would place their car in a pit stop for a time penalty. The reward for finishing the race included a letter home to parents.

Another colleague used an individual snake as a more private method of reward. Each time a target was met a segment of the snake was coloured in. Once the snake was completed a reward was given. It is important that the reward is tailored to the individual. One child in the class was given the opportunity to access the Internet and email his favourite footballer when he had reached a learning target – a powerful incentive to achieve.

Praise should not be difficult to gain. It should relate to individual or group success, and it should be regular, timely, specific and given with sincerity. When praise meets these criteria it will support the child who needs regular and precise positive reinforcement. Many teachers will recognise such children; at the end of a lesson, having tried their best and achieved the implicit goals that a teacher requires, the child will ask the teacher, 'Have I been good?'

Praise that is universal and unconditional soon becomes transparent, it does not indicate where success has taken place, and only serves to devalue the universal currency of praise itself. A regular and specific praise feedback rate is another quality of a teacher in the learning zone. Teachers should not underestimate the reassurance, impact and value of their praise.

Sutton (1991) reminds us that assessment is a form of communication. Teachers who work in a setting where they mark children's work can use this form of communication to great benefit. They can give a clear indication of what is good about the work at the same time as setting targets for improvement. For those children who experience severe learning difficulties the augmentative systems, such as the use of symbols, photographs or objects of reference (Park 1997), may be necessary in order to communicate progress.

Use sanctions positively

Sanctions are a necessary component of a school behaviour policy and are most likely to involve the removal of perceived privileges. Some schools employ a tariff system that involves an incremental taxonomy of sanctions – if you break a rule, it immediately results in a pre-determined sanction. This system has its limitations. For example, what should a school do in relation to acts of violence? Should a punch in the nose result in a detention, causing nosebleed produce a letter home, and breaking a nose mean a fixed-term exclusion?

This somewhat flippant example points to a more serious problem. A system of taxonomy contradicts an ethos that aims to meet individual needs. How should a special school react when a young pupil with severe and complex learning difficulties presses the fire alarm because of the sensory stimulation involved in bell ringing and the enormous cause and effect response that empties the whole building? Sanctions must take the individual context and needs of a child into account. A behaviour policy should maintain a clear relationship between rewards and sanctions – my preference would be for an imbalance that is substantially in favour of rewards.

Use the 'catch them being good' method

When I completed my teacher training, I was unleashed upon the unsuspecting pupils as a qualified member of the 'ton of bricks' brigade. I was somehow conditioned to think that I could only sustain a relaxed, friendly but assertive relationship with the pupils by reacting aggressively at the first sign of a misdemeanour. It was good practice to search out the first offending culprit in a class and to come down upon them in a loud and unmerciful torrent of cold-blooded threat. The rationale behind this practice was that a public demonstration of your ability to frighten children would inevitably teach them that you were not to be messed with. An underlying principle of establishing such 'discipline' was that the pupils might have to fear you before they begin to respect you. The skilled disciplinarian would hit the first offender hard and other potential offenders would learn to keep their distance.

Classroom experience soon taught me that that the 'catch them being good' method is a far more productive and respectful means of promoting positive behaviour. A teacher who consistently adopts the 'catch them being bad' method might be in the ludicrous position of criticising a lack of politeness by using impolite and disrespectful behaviour. The use of sanctions as revenge, or over-corrective retribution, is a feature of the battle zone. It only serves to encourage pupils to invent methods of ensuring that they do not get caught breaking rules. They are not involved in a process where they learn and understand the necessity for specific rules and the reasons why they should not be broken. There has to be a place for sanctions in the learning zone as long as they are applied fairly and respectfully and are seen as part of the learning process.

Use tactical concentration

'Tactical ignoring' is a phrase used to describe a sanction that is used to send messages to children about positive behaviour. A child will receive absence of attention for low level disruptive behaviour and will notice others being rewarded for positive on-task behaviour. It can also be applied to children who present high level challenging behaviour. However, safety must be paramount when tactical ignoring is being used, because prolonged tactical ignoring can be a danger when a child is increasing the possibility and potential for harm and damage.

One of my colleagues would say during tactical ignoring 'Who can I say well done to for...?' and then describe the specific behaviour that she required. She would reward each child with her praise, and the pupil who was presenting challenging behaviour would not be rewarded until they were doing exactly as she described. When the pupil eventually did as requested she would thank them. Although I have used the phrase tactical ignoring, it is in fact a misnomer because it does not involve ignoring at all. The phrase 'tactical concentration' gives a better indication of the complex skills of observation and concentration, which are disguised as ignoring. The use of tactical concentration can demonstrate that the absence of reward is a very effective sanction.

Sanctions need not cause irreparable damage to a positive and responsive relationship between a pupil and a teacher. A teacher should not be concerned about saying 'I'm sorry, you have broken a rule and that means that you have to . . . .' The positive and respectful use of sanctions will promote solutions and ensures that the integrity and dignity of the pupil, and the teacher, remain intact.

Demolish the 'naughty chair'

The use of a naughty chair, a naughty mat, or a naughty corner, is an intervention that is commonly used for young children. This strategy reinforces a non-interactive view of the causation of a behaviour difficulty. It tells a child – *you* are naughty, and this is the place for naughty children just like *you*. The child's interpretation of this personal intervention will be that she or he is a 'bad' person and the place to which they have been banished is for bad children like them. It presents a restrictive and fixed notion of behaviour being locked within children and does not offer any opportunity to focus on the influential role of the learning environment.

Such a strategy also removes the focus from a specific behaviour onto the child as a person. The naughty chair tells a child that they are good at being bad. I accept that this type of disengagement strategy can be very successful, but I would recommend that 'naughty' places be renamed 'thinking' places. The teacher can disengage a child by telling them to go to a certain place and think about their *behaviour*. The use of a 'thinking chair' is positive and respectful to children.

When things seem to be going wrong

Positive behaviour can be established at the start of a lesson through a variety of means. The teacher should arrive before the pupils and organise their entry. Pupils who are used to a culture of morning and afternoon registration will respond to the learned and expected behaviours associated with such a time. Using a register at the start of a lesson can formalise learning and provide an explicit indication of the standards of behaviour that are required before learning can take place.

Other factors that promote positive behaviour relate to the working environment. The teacher must be clear about teaching and learning intentions, and the pupils should be told what they are expected to do and why they are doing it. Individual relevance should be evident through the process of differentiation. Adopting a range of teaching styles will match the variety of learning styles in a classroom. This avoids a situation where the continual use of one teaching style reinforces the learning anonymity of a child and makes them feel like a failure.

Even when classrooms are positive and purposeful there will be times when challenging behaviour occurs. Adopting positive strategies can equip the teacher and the pupil with a way out of such potentially difficult situations. The following strategies feature in the learning zone because they enable the teacher and the pupil to continue to develop new skills during times that can be both stressful and distressing.

Prevent free theatre

When challenging behaviour occurs it may be exacerbated by the presence of an audience. It should never be allowed to become a form of undignified free theatre. When a teacher identifies a pupil who presents low level disruptive behaviour they can use a phrase such as 'We will discuss this after the lesson.' There are times during challenging behaviour when the removal of the child from the audience will decrease a difficulty and increase the safety of everyone involved. There may also be times when a challenging behaviour is judged to be of a severity and intensity that it requires the audience to be removed from the child. In such situations, the class is removed leaving the child without an audience. A child presenting this type of behaviour should not be left alone when in a distressed state. Care should be taken to observe with discretion and sensitivity from a suitable distance.

The adult will make a professional judgement about the best time to re-engage with a child by observing such elements as the way in which a child's breathing is slowing down and the content of what the child is saying. McGee *et al.* (1987) describe a person-centred model of intervention which involves interruption, redirection and reward. The adult will intervene and redirect the child's attention onto something else that can gain a positive response. The skilful and consistent application of such a paradigm can prevent challenging behaviour from becoming a distasteful public performance with mutual loss of dignity.

Reject the behaviour and respect the person

A teacher must see a behaviour difficulty as a learning difficulty and accept the significance of the interaction between the child and the learning environment in creating challenging behaviour. This prevents the teacher from blaming a child for their negative behaviour and making personal comments to the child such as 'The trouble with *you* is . . . .' A teacher must also set high standards and expectations of what a pupil can learn. A clear definition of acceptable and unacceptable behaviour must operate in the classroom and the school.

It is possible to help pupils learn how to change their behaviour by being precise about their undesired behaviour. This is a skill that involves separating the child from their behaviour and focusing on intended positive behaviours. A teacher can criticise the behaviour without making the child feel that they are disliked. When this happens the child receives a positive message that says – I do not like your *behaviour* when you do that, I cannot let you do that in my classroom, but I still like you. The use of a child's name followed by a description of desired or undesired behaviour should be used as an indicator that the teacher sees a child as separate from their behaviour. The child is accepted and respected but the behaviour is fundamentally rejected.

Use positive descriptors

When intervening in a challenging situation, a teacher can remember the positive qualities of the child and use positive descriptors. Previous positive information can be used to reduce challenging behaviour. A teacher might say, 'I know that you are really reliable and now I want to rely upon you to…', explaining a desired behaviour. In a situation where conflict is taking place, the teacher can remind the child of what they are like when they are not presenting a challenge and ask for specific positive behaviour.

The element of conflict is reduced when a teacher intervenes and describes the behaviour that they desire by saying 'I want you to…' This tells the child *what they have to do* and how they can do it. For those children who do not have the skills to find their way out of a difficulty, this provides a positive exit sign.

If the teacher says, 'I do not want you to....', it might indicate that they are entering the battle zone. The child knows what they are *not* supposed to do and may continue doing it in order to create a win–lose situation. Using positive descriptors can help the teacher to be responsive rather than reactive to challenging behaviour.

This approach can also be used in the time after a challenging behaviour has taken place. Some children will feel upset and distressed about what they have done and the teacher should aim to find a positive outcome for the child. This provides opportunities for the child to be involved in changing their behaviour. A teacher might say 'I know that you were angry and dangerous, but you only took two minutes to calm down and do as you were asked. That is a big improvement because when this used to happen before, it could take as long as fifteen minutes for you to calm yourself down.' The focus can then move onto the challenging behaviour itself. Positive information from a mediator of change can enable a child to understand that they are making a change.

Avoid bouncing

There are times when a teacher makes a reasonable request and a pupil turns it into a declaration of war. A simple request such as 'Can you please not talk when I am talking' can be seen as an opportunity for a pupil to involve a teacher in a protracted debate. This debate will only occur if the teacher allows it to, by failing to spot that an element of bouncing is imminent. The pupil might respond by denying that they were talking and blame somebody else instead. The teacher may then insist that the teacher is right because they saw the pupil talk. It is possible that the teacher will raise their voice in anger. From this point the teacher is being bounced into the battle zone.

The pupil can raise the stakes and tell the teacher not to shout. The teacher enters an argument about status, and questions how the child dares to make such a comment. A sanction is issued. Instead of being flexible, the teacher continues bouncing. The pupil might slam a book on the desk claiming that the sanction is not fair. The teacher will then argue about slamming books on desks, the necessity for property to be respected, and the importance of school rules. The threat of a different sanction is then introduced.

This escalating public battle scenario continues. A skilled pupil may aim to involve their peers in the debate in order to create the battle-zone version of teacher pinball. The teacher will have been bouncing about in between pupil behaviour and each bounce moves them further away from the reason for the initial intervention.

This can also happen in a special school setting with a child who has limited communication and experiences severe learning difficulties. The style of intervention and the child's response can create a situation where the teacher is bounced around between different forms of challenging behaviour, responding at an ever-increasing rate. A teacher has to be aware of their bounce potential because the battle zone is over-populated by bouncing teachers.

Avoid instruction clutter

In a situation where there is potential conflict the teacher should make demands and requests that are specific and clear. In the heat of the moment, there is a tendency to abandon one simple instruction and to confuse pupils with a complex list of behaviours that they must comply with. This restricts resolution, especially if the teacher has not checked whether the child has heard and processed the first instruction. When children are angry and upset, active listening is not their greatest skill. The teacher should give a clear priority instruction that acknowledges the pupil's feelings and tell them what they should be doing. 'I can see that you are really upset, but I want you to stop shouting and swearing so that we can solve this problem together.'

A teacher should not replicate an aspect of the undesired behaviour – shouting competitions will not eliminate shouting. In such a case a teacher should speak quietly and say to the child 'Listen to me (pause), I am not shouting, (pause) I want you to talk to me like I am talking to you.' There should be recognition of the priority instruction being met, 'Thank you. Now that you have stopped shouting and swearing, we can begin to . . . .' Changing behaviour is part of the learning process and as we give children ample time to demonstrate their learning, we should also give them sufficient time to react to an initial instruction. This can be done by the use of the phrase 'When you are ready, I would like you to...'

McNamara and Moreton (1995) refer to the 'broken record technique' that emphasises the need for the teacher to describe their demand over and over again so that the behaviour of the pupil can change. Avoiding instruction clutter will support a range of children – those who are self-injurious, those who challenge the teacher with 'in your face' behaviour and those who present persistent behaviour that offers a subtle enticement into the outer regions of the battle zone.

Focus on teaching

Some pupils find teaching and learning to be a painful experience that re-inforces their low self-esteem and challenges their limited tedium threshold. Some of these pupils develop a sophisticated armoury of skills aimed at hijacking and cancelling the teaching and learning process. It is important that the teacher asserts their role within the classroom and does not become diverted by pupil techniques that are geared towards the postponement of teaching and the negation of a teacher's role. In such a situation, a pupil or group of pupils may try to change the lesson agenda so that teaching is abandoned and the class indulges in a lengthy and wide-ranging discussion about behaviour instead.

Become a supermodel

One aspect of the art of teaching is to continually model the behaviour that you desire from the pupils. This skill becomes extremely important whenever a teacher intervenes in a challenging situation. A teacher that remains calm will model self-control and will avoid an escalation of conflict. The calm teacher will be aware of their own physiological reaction to a challenging situation and this places them in a position from which they can focus on resolution. It is hard for a pupil to 'fight' with someone who refuses to be enticed or seduced by the opening gambits of an argument.

A teacher who consistently models respectful behaviour will always be in an advantageous position if they encounter challenging behaviour. Such a teacher can say, 'Please do not speak to me like that, I never speak to you like that', or 'Please do not be disrespectful towards me, I am never disrespectful towards you.' The child will respond as long as the teacher's statement is actually true! If a child with learning difficulties is kicking or hitting a teacher, the same rule applies. The teacher can say, or sign, 'Please do not hit me, I never do that to you and I'm not doing it to you now' (the implicit message being 'even though you are doing it to me'). In difficult times it is always possible to reap the rewards of a positive and respectful relationship with a child.

Choose your zone

Figure 5.1 indicates two sequential pathways of intervention that are available in each zone. At the core of the battle zone teachers can be confrontational and disrespectful. They provide children with confusing or condescending messages that can make a child feel worthless or powerless. They have fixed responses to challenging situations and their unwillingness to take each individual context into account will often cause conflict. A teacher intervening in the battle zone may be prone to responding to behaviours that pupils use to set the teacher bouncing. These pupils may try to gain peer recognition for their behaviour or they might lure and manipulate the teacher into an escalation of mounting difficulties. The teacher will intervene, determined that

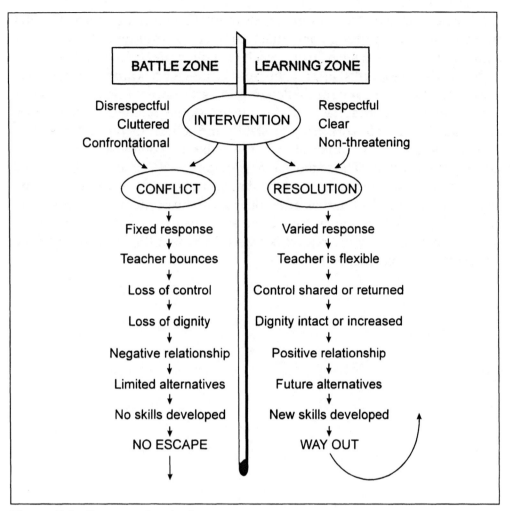

Figure 5.1   Intervention paths

they have to win the battle, and the resolution of a problem is replaced by a full-blown confrontation. This situation provides negative relationship patterns and offers no opportunities for the mutual development of new skills. It also increases stress levels because there never seems to be a way out.

At the core of the learning zone teachers are respectful and responsive. They provide children with clear and consistent messages that cannot be perceived as threatening. Their flexible responses prevent them from bouncing and provide them with an ability to focus on problem solving. They offer a child the way out of a difficulty. They promote positive relationship patterns and offer dignified opportunities for the mutual development of new skills. The teacher has the power to decide the zone to which they will belong.

If teachers are expected to promote positive behaviour, and work within the framework of the learning zone, there must be recognition of the complex emotional impact that such an approach to challenging behaviour has upon staff. To adopt respectful approaches and strategies towards children who present the complete range of challenging and self-injurious behaviour places a requirement upon some staff to unlearn some of their own learned behaviour. When staff work in a consistently and coherently positive way they will need support. Such an approach is exacting and demands the constant development of skills. The school has to provide specific time for professional development and teacher support for staff as individuals and as a team. The support itself must be relative, and relevant, to the particular school setting and pupil population. The process of meeting the needs of the 'whole child' becomes more successful in a working environment that aims to meet the needs of the 'whole teacher' too.

Chapter 6

Review and reflection: a school-based system for support and development

Teachers' need for support

Teaching is an intellectually and physically demanding occupation that can be made more effective and efficient when the school accepts the common, distinct and individual needs of the teachers as well as those of the children. The stream of government initiatives arriving in schools over the past decade has placed immense pressure upon teachers to change. Teachers have been bombarded by linear concepts of progress, attainment defined within the parameters of 'normal' cognitive development and an overloaded curriculum. Externally enforced change, particularly when it seems to ceaselessly cascade down from a non-consultative hierarchical structure, will inevitably demoralise those who are expected to implement the change. It also erodes and undermines the concept of professional judgement.

I am not arguing for the abandonment of external or internal accountability in schools. Accountability is vital in the quest to improve standards for every child in the education system. I am stating that teaching and learning are dynamic processes and teachers should be involved in shaping national, regional and school-based change. Erosion of professional integrity will not encourage any teacher to contribute or respond to change.

The responsibility of school managers

Teaching is also a potentially stressful occupation, but teachers and support staff do not have to be stressed by it. This is particularly important in an environment where there is a high proportion of children who present challenging behaviour, such as an SLD, EBD or increasingly, an MLD school. I have asserted that children who are educated in a special school should expect to receive something special and distinct out of it – the same principle must apply to the staff in those schools. The school management has a responsibility to ensure that a special school can identify elements of its practice that make it 'special' for the staff. In this context, the term 'special' refers to an acceptance that a distinct population of children will create a distinct set of needs amongst the staff. School managers must be responsive to those needs.

The role of a school manager, in a school where children present challenging behaviour, must include the willingness to develop systems that recognise the needs of the staff. This includes developing systems that operate in a proactive manner so that stress can be prevented or reduced. There is an argument that head teachers, and their deputies, can only truly understand the needs of teachers who work in stressful situations if they actually teach in those situations themselves. National initiatives have made it particularly difficult for head teachers to plan their time so that they can remain in teaching contact with the children, although many do.

As a consequence, a greater responsibility is placed upon the deputy head teacher to commit their time to teaching, and to support colleagues when difficulties emerge in their classrooms. Teachers will wish to discuss pedagogical issues with their deputy, such as how to plan curriculum activities so that they provide a match between learning need and learning provision. This process is more likely to take place when the deputy aims to provide a model of good teaching practice. It is less likely to take place if colleagues feel that the deputy has little teaching contact with the children. In a world of labels, the assumption made about a head *teacher* and deputy head *teacher* is that they are particularly skilled in the art of teaching. Their colleagues will assume or expect that they can learn about teaching from them.

Managing tensions

A management team that offers leadership will not neglect the needs of its staff as human beings with a life beyond school as well as in it. Gersch (1996) emphasises that teachers are not immune from symptoms of stress such as loss of motivation, irritability, depression, feeling tense and feeling negative about where and how they work. A positive school-based support system can prevent the appearance or advancement of such symptoms. A teacher should not have to be in a position where they feel that they cannot face going to work because of the invisibility or lack of interest of a school support system that has not picked up the early warning signals. The situation is made worse if the teacher has requested support but not received it. In this context, the 'sickie' day is often not an indication of a medical ailment but a description of feelings brought on by stress. 'I'm sick', can be interpreted as 'I'm sick of the difficulties I experience in isolation and the lack of support that I am receiving.' A supportive school will offer staff opportunities to talk about their feelings and to express their opinions even if they challenge the school's structures and processes.

Creative management of competing ideologies and perspectives will enable a school to embark upon a shared journey without anyone feeling that the expression of a contentious idea will either compromise them, or force them to be thrown overboard. A critical voice might present fundamental challenges to school philosophy but it can be used to strengthen a desire to move forward. When staff aim to achieve explicit collective and individual goals their mutual and individual integrity has to be respected. Such an open approach has to be supported by open classrooms where staff and children can work collaboratively.

Multi-sensory support

A school should provide systems that are responsive to the needs of individual staff and pupils. This can be done when colleagues meet together regularly to review the systems and structures within the school and to reflect upon their practice and responsibility within them. The process of reflection provides a system for mutual support through the sharing of skills, strategies, feelings and difficulties. An acceptance of a difficulty is a positive step – a teacher should never feel that it is going to be interpreted as the acknowledgement of a failure. When difficulties are identified they should be followed by a collective interest in finding solutions.

The actual existence of a system that claims to support staff is not enough because being supported is a multi-sensory experience that extends beyond systems provision. Teachers should feel supported; they should see evidence of support, and hear that those who are offering support are doing so in a non-judgmental fashion. For many teachers, being supported is less about the state of the working environment, and more about their own state of mind.

A school-based system for support should have the consensus and power to review and implement agreed change. It should provide an organisational challenge to staff who listen to the talk about change but allow it to pass over their own classroom. A support system that meets the needs of teachers will combat this 'passover principle' and can add to the general quality of change itself. Such a collaborative problem-solving system could be described as school-based 'review and reflection'.

The benefits of review and reflection

Formal meetings in a school have an agenda that is set by external or internal demands, requirements, and pressures. Informal meetings often create their own very different agendas. In an informal setting, teachers talk about their working conditions and may take the opportunity to complain to each other. The informal context enables anecdotes to be related, contentious issues to be debated, and may produce a more honest and open atmosphere.

Teachers will talk of their successes: lessons that went well, a child who achieved something particular that day, planning that worked, or an idea that they are proud of. They will talk about the frustrations, concerns and difficulties involved in their day to day working. They will also share stories and laugh together – the collective sense of humour is often a powerful support system in a potentially stressful working environment.

This openness is stifled in a formal setting which is based on a structure that can be both hierarchical, and gender- and culture-biased. The hierarchical setting can prevent some staff from participating because they are anxious that a constructive contribution can be interpreted as a criticism. The potential for management revenge can inhibit contributions. Yet, when teachers meet out of school it will only be a short time before someone is accused of 'talking shop' and a little longer before the practice becomes infectious.

Formalise the informal

So why do we do behave so differently in different contexts? There will be reasons related to the codes, conventions, and dynamics of informal contexts but my contention is that one reason is because our working environments do not allow teachers to formalise the positive elements of informal settings. There are few opportunities in a school year for staff to be given time to investigate and understand their developing role in their own workplace. To create such a forum requires a flexible structure with a radical approach to agenda setting and the allocation of 'directed time'. It also requires an approach to school management, which accepts that personal and professional development in an eclectic working environment will be most effective when conflicts and tensions are accepted as part of the conditions for change.

The process of change and development must be continuous if 'review and reflection' is to improve teaching and learning conditions. This involves reviewing the school's organisational systems, aims, ethos and classroom processes and reflecting upon their improvement. It also involves supporting staff in the type of day to day work that can build up individual stress and reduce collective morale. Low staff morale, and a depressed collective self-image, will never enable a school to improve the self-esteem of the children who learn within it.

Even though the Elton Report (1989) suggested that systems for teacher peer support would be beneficial, it still remains more common for teachers to look for external support rather than instituting their own. For those primary and secondary schools that are considering the introduction of a teacher support team, the work of Creese *et al.* (1997) provides an excellent rationale and practical methods for the creation of such a group. Whilst an improvement in the quality of teaching and learning should be an intended outcome in any school, there are needs that individual teachers express in a special school that highlight their specific working conditions. Examples of these might include dealing with regular verbal abuse, being physically attacked, experiencing a child's self-injurious behaviour, supporting a child in coming to terms with a physical disability, or coping with a relationship with a child who has a limited life expectancy. A mainstream model of teacher support needs adaptation for the individual and distinct contexts of a special school setting.

Review and reflection – getting started

I would like to present a brief account of the introduction of a 'review and reflection' support group at Alexandra School. I shall write about it from my perspective as a deputy head teacher who was involved in designing the model and who participated as a group member. Alexandra School, an all-age school for children with emotional and behavioural difficulties was identified as a 'failing' school and was in need of enormous institutional change. It was evident that there was a need for supporting staff in raising the standard of teaching and learning. The new management team accepted that the need for support related to every member of staff who worked in and through the school.

A group was established which aimed at creating an environment where staff could support each other as a team and as individuals. The title 'review and reflection' was chosen because the group envisaged two main features of its focus: 'reviewing' school systems and 'reflecting' upon teaching and learning. It was seen as a group that would make us as effective as possible in implementing change in these areas.

Special schools can be insular and isolationist. They can become defensive about the outside world's perception and understanding of 'their' children. They can also allow themselves to become precious and protective, which detaches them from a distinct role in national educational provision. Special educators should not assume that they are the sole experts on the learning needs of children who experience special educational needs simply because they work in the same building as them every day. They should also not allow themselves to be victims of their architectural and town planning inheritance. I will allow the reader to make their own judgements about why so many special schools seem to be hidden behind trees or large buildings, or are only accessible through long driveways that are difficult to locate. Combating isolationism involves recognition that staff in special schools need to develop their outreach role. This involves opening the school out to the wider community instead of protecting it from perceived external contamination.

In changing a demoralised environment it has to be accepted that outside agencies are not a threat and that they can offer guidance and support. Alexandra sought such external guidance from an 'academic' institution when considering the development of a structure for its review and reflection group. The caricature of aloof academics, detached from reality, living in ivory towers, must be challenged if schools are to receive the valuable and insightful support that can be offered by academic teams and individuals.

Positive and negative factors in implementing a support group

The staff approached the notion of review and reflection with enthusiasm because it recognised their needs within a demanding and stressful environment. It also created a context for support and change. The staff identified the advantages and disadvantages of such a group. They saw possible benefits in areas such as the reduction of stress; the opportunity to be respected as people; the sharing of problems, and recognising that others encounter the same difficulties. They felt that the group could also provide an arena for developing new coping strategies and experimental approaches to teaching.

One of the major benefits was the potential to create a culture where staff did not feel judged or blamed if children presented challenging behaviour. The aim was to strengthen staff as teachers and as people. The children attended the school for a reason and their complex needs might present complex difficulties in the learning environment. The development of resilience and strength enables staff to adopt a flexible and sensitive approach towards children who experience emotional and behavioural learning difficulties and present challenging behaviour. Being consistently positive can be exhausting.

The disadvantages included a realistic concern about whether it was possible to create a status-free zone that included people whom the system labelled deputy or head teacher. A horizontal model of shared management and leadership could only be implemented if the group remained aware and honest about the effect that status would have upon it. The alternative was a suspicious undercurrent that the school managers had a different agenda from the rest of the group. No matter how collegiate a school claims to be it still operates within a system where status exists and affects the decision-making process. The optimal condition was to accept that status beyond the group would impinge upon the group and to aim for a climate of suspended status.

There were also concerns about creating a group where people might regret saying something because of an anxiety that someone might use it against them at a later date. When a school is labelled as 'failing' or under 'special measures' every member of staff feels let down. This may cause some to become defensive and others to feel that an overall damning judgement of the school has nullified their own conscientious individual efforts.

The size of the group, which was no larger than twelve staff, made it manageable. A ceiling of fifteen was identified to be the point at which consideration would be given to creating two distinct groups. The separation of the staff into two groups was seen as a potentially negative factor and this could be an issue for a larger special school that was considering adopting a teacher support model. The positive aspects of creating a group with a focus on problem-coping and problem-solving outweighed the negatives. The staff decided to set up the group. To ensure that review and reflection would not be a problem-creating group, the process of rule setting began with all members defining priority rules in order to achieve a consensus.

Setting ground rules: it is not a 'moaning monster'

A focus of review and reflection was placed on working within the school. It would be perfectly acceptable in this context for a member of staff to raise issues that had implications for the management of the school. The school had to make immediate change and in this group the systems were to be the focus of scrutiny and discussion – not the people. Previous systems needed restructuring and those that did not improve the children's ability to learn had to be laid to rest. This was not always universally popular action to take. Such decisions often raised the tensions of 'therapy or teaching?' that exist in the great EBD debate. Review and reflection was a setting in which anyone could raise these issues without feeling that there would be a negative management response if they were not seen to be toeing the party line.

The group aimed to support staff in making sense of institutional changes some of which were swift, imperative and may have been perceived as chaotic or perplexing. These changes affected all adults and therefore the group was open to any adult who worked in the school and who volunteered to attend. One member of the teaching staff exercised her right not to participate in the group. She was invited to join at the start of each term but declined to do so. Efforts were made to keep her informed of broad areas of group discussion although our agreement in terms of confidentiality meant that we did not talk about specific comments made by individuals. Similar feedback about the content of each meeting was displayed in the staff room for all colleagues to see. This enabled them to be informed and to ask for particular suggestions or support in any of the topics that were covered. It was important to ensure that the group did not develop into a clique by alienating those colleagues who could not or chose not to attend. The teacher who did not join the group moved to a new school within a year and from that point in time all future teaching staff were group members.

The practicalities of domestic arrangements made it difficult for many learning assistants to attend although some were able to make a regular commitment. All of the part-time members of the teaching staff attended. The meetings took place within a teacher's hours of directed time and those learning assistants who wished to attend had their working hours changed accordingly. The status afforded to the group by its inclusion into directed time was a method of identifying that this was something 'special' for staff who worked in this particular special school. Teaching staff who chose not to attend were expected to remain in school, using their directed time in a different way.

Due to the nature and purpose of the school, it was expected that emotional matters would be discussed, but the focus would always be on a personal response to professional experiences. It was not an organisational structure for group counselling and psychotherapy. Most importantly it was not, and never should become, a moaning monster. The following rules were agreed and set:

- Confidentiality will be paramount.

- The group is for giving to others as well as receiving from them.

- There is an expectation of commitment.

- Colleagues will be positive and respectful towards each other.

- An emphasis on the positive will not prevent matters that are perceived as negative from being discussed – but positive outcomes and solutions will be sought.

- The group accepts the need to evaluate its purpose, and success, at regular intervals.

Organisation

The group met every two weeks for sessions that lasted for 45 minutes. New members were invited at the start of each new term. There was a large amount of discussion about the need for a group facilitator. It was decided that an external facilitator might not be able to grasp the issues associated with working in such specialist provision for children who are experiencing such complex emotional, behavioural and associated learning difficulties. The team of staff that constituted the first review and reflection group decided that two facilitators should be chosen from within the school. One was a class teacher and another a part-time member of staff. These two members of staff received external supervision that was paid for by the school and were happy to take on such a role.

It was agreed that there would be no agenda for the meetings but that the facilitators would take responsibility for gentle direction of issues when this seemed necessary. This involved the facilitators deploying their skills in enabling staff to receive a fair share of time, or intervening if they felt that an emerging tension needed managing. Such tensions were never about people or personalities. They were more often about individual stances on philosophy, pedagogy or curriculum content. With a focus on problem solving, the group operated within its agreed aims, to support each other in the process of becoming more reflective and effective practitioners. This enabled the school to take the fast track towards its own 'zone of proximal development'! (Vygotsky 1978)

Content

The group did not specify a content for the meetings. However, there was one occasion when it was agreed that the facilitators could specify content. This session brought tensions about the function and purpose of the group to the surface. One member of staff wanted the agenda to remain within the boundaries of school systems and curriculum while another was more interested in exploring the psychosocial aspects of his role. The tension between practical review in relation to the school, and reflecting on feelings that may be separate from the school, was often evident and always accepted. It was seen as a method of promoting formative discussion about how school improvement could be achieved in a group setting where there was an equitable value given to competing viewpoints and expectations.

Open discussion also involved staff in the debate about achieving a shared vision within a complex interaction of personal and institutional work models. The suspension of status within the group was a liberating experience for staff who wished to speak honestly about they way that they felt when they were involved in challenging situations. Those structures that reinforce rigid hierarchical status are more likely to be ice-makers than ice-breakers.

Relevant issues

A wide variety of relevant issues were discussed. These included discussions about the ethics of administering Ritalin to pupils, how staff cope with the loss of children who are taken into foster care in another part of the country, the difference between pressure and stress in our own working environment, and the function and purpose of special schools. There was discussion about our responses to those children whose childhood has been brutally cut short at an early age. There was also discussion about the anxieties that an adult might have about losing self-control when they are in a situation that is physically threatening.

Invisible or abusive parents

Some of the parents at the school had been physically threatening and others had been verbally abusive to staff. The review and reflection group explored the reasons why some parents might react in this way, while others would support the school. For some parents there is an element of guilt and resentment when their child is 'sent' to a special school. For others their own experience of schooling makes any school a daunting place that renders them powerless. The school had to respond to parents who felt disempowered, by trying to understand how they felt – they were an important factor in changing the quality of education that the school was offering. Hornby (1995) presents a model for parental involvement that emphasises the importance of parental expertise and contribution in a collaborative partnership. This partnership is more difficult to achieve when parents feel resentful towards the stigmatisation of special school placement and have a limited range of strategies for expressing concern or anger to perceived authority figures.

A real partnership between parents and the school will share power and respect and have a direct effect on the quality of learning. It will also provide a structure for reinforcing the aims of the school. The group investigated parental need rather than reacting to parental difficulties. Staff aimed at remaining sensitive to parental reasons for the rejection of special provision and the group recommended a programme of parental visits for lunch with the pupils. This was the first step in encouraging parents into classrooms and to convincing them they were a vital part of the changes that were taking place. The parent–teacher relationship must operate in the best interests of children (Wolfendale 1992).

Our record of achievement

The mutual sharing of perspectives enabled the group to continue to present ideas to the school management team, and to have a direct influence upon the content and implementation of the school development plan. The meetings were developing into an organic structure for staff-directed professional development. Meetings also focused on the positive aspect of our work in the classroom. One meeting was structured so that each member of staff talked about one positive thing that had happened to them in that week. In another meeting we reflected upon a past term and completed our own record of achievement as a school.

In a stressful environment, recognition of positive achievements among the staff is vital in boosting morale. Teachers should recognise the small steps of progress that they are making in school in the same way that they do for the children. As a profession, we do not spend enough time praising or complimenting each other on our practice. Emerging needs also determined topics that were discussed. There were meetings about children who present self-injurious behaviour, and consideration of how we support our colleagues when we see a situation where they might be in physical danger.

The return of the inspectors
The review and reflection group was invaluable as the process of school inspection drew nearer. The school had been removed from the 'failing' list and when the school underwent re-inspection, every member of staff wanted to demonstrate the enormous changes that had taken place. The impending inspection was often a topic for discussion and staff were able to talk about their anxieties. There was a feeling that we were 'all in it together for the pupils', and this collegial support prompted a meeting where each teacher talked about what they do, why they do it, and re-affirmed that they were good at it. A school has to be accountable for the standard and quality of learning that takes place within it and this group enabled every teacher to articulate their own contribution to raising standards.

This analytical and self-critical group became a school-based system for personal resource development and the building of self-confidence. Not surprisingly, the meeting that took place during inspection week was an opportunity for people to talk about their experiences, and to receive a self-esteem boost from their colleagues. The inspection outcomes were very successful ones, but even this did not prevent the feeling of anti-climax that occurs afterwards. When the inspectors disappear over the unbroken horizon, the school has to cope with the emotional response of the debilitated and drained members of its community – staff and pupils. Review and reflection supported the school through the excited high and exhausted low that followed the inspection.

Evaluation of school-based support

It had been agreed that the group would involve itself in a process of internal evaluation before it sought external qualitative evaluation. A meeting was set aside to reflect upon the purpose and direction of the group and each member of staff identified what they saw as its aims and successes. The following selection of responses covers some of the staff contributions:

- learning how to respond to difficulties by sharing what happened
- reducing my own stress levels
- solving potential headaches
- a calm time to reflect before I go home – it makes home life better
- discussing different staff philosophies
- meeting my own individual needs
- sharing positive and stressful experiences in a confidential environment
- you get a voice and you are actually taken seriously – it makes a difference to how you feel
- increasing my confidence and ability to relax in the classroom
- some silence and stillness amongst the constant noise of school
- looking at issues from different viewpoints
- offering my ideas to others in a supportive way
- improving my ability to plan how I will react in difficult situations
- understanding challenging behaviour so that I can be better at my job
- a secure base from which to build relationships with colleagues whom you hardly see in the busy atmosphere of a special school.

It can be seen that the group met distinct needs of the staff as well as their individual needs. Some staff identified that the group was most useful for sharing ideas and strategies. Others felt that it gave an impetus and confirmation to the new vision that the school was implementing. Some found that it gave them time to recognise their own physiological response to a potentially stressful working environment. It was also seen as an opportunity for the staff to get to know each other as individuals rather than solely as professionals.

It was clear that an innovative structure for school-based support, that accepted and confronted the inherent philosophical and ideological tensions in the education of children with such complex learning needs, was proving to be beneficial at a variety of levels. It supported staff through a period of change as well as increasing their knowledge, understanding, and commitment to the implementation of the change. It also increased the corporate skills and knowledge base, which could be used as a resource to improve learning.

Review and reflection also provided a system through which staff received constructive support and advice from each other. Such a system acknowledges and rewards the work of those who offer support and advice.

One of the major outcomes of the 'reflection' element of the group was the mutual trust that developed amongst staff. There was an increased willingness for staff to experiment with new practice and to share its rewards and frustrations. Although staff were given the chance to join or leave the group at the end of each term, the only time a colleague left was if they moved to a post in a different school.

A major outcome of the process of 'review' was to implement new systems and adapt or reject old systems and procedures. Children who present challenging behaviour need to be given a fresh start every day. This is more likely in a working environment that supports the teacher in making a fresh start too. The ultimate focus of review and reflection was to improve the learning environment and learning potential for every pupil in the school.

The continuation of review and reflection

The review and reflection group is still a purposeful and powerful forum for the staff at Alexandra School. Once the initial major changes and innovations were implemented, and staff felt more confident in their ability to teach children who find it difficult to learn, further evaluation took place. The staff decided that their needs were now different and decided to meet once every three weeks. There was a group discussion, initiated by the facilitators, about the complexities of being part of the group as well as having a defined role within it. The facilitators asked for a trial period where they could be released from their role. The group continued without facilitators and has kept this structure since.

For such a system to be successful it must be directed by the needs of the staff in the complex contexts in which they work. There came a time when the group met once a month, but a recent influx of new staff has prompted a further consideration of the timing and structure of review and reflection. Since the group began, every new member of the teaching staff has chosen to join the group and to stay a member of it. New staff need time to embed themselves into the learning culture of a particular school and to share concerns and successes – review and reflection provides a system in which this can happen.

This brief descriptive example highlights the possibilities for special schools in providing collaborative and reflective school-based support for their staff. In a special school environment time is valuable and precious. Planning-time during the day is at a minimum, and can be lost due to the absence of one member of staff. For staff to work as effectively as possible on behalf of the children they must be given time to do so. Quality time will improve the quality of teaching and learning in the school. School managers have to be creative in finding time where staff can talk to each other in a setting where management is about motivation not manipulation. A school-based support system such as review and reflection offers such opportunities for personal and professional development.

I am aware that this model of review and reflection cannot be generalised to every special school, as each school has to take into account its own context, and needs. I have described this process, and included staff responses, in an attempt to promote discussion about how a learning organisation can support the development of learning among its staff as well as its pupils. Every school has teachers with different experiences, ideologies and perspectives and should confront the issues of how a culture of 'review' and 'reflection' can become a tool for improvement, innovation, support, development, and change.

A positive postscript

Figure 6.1 illustrates a framework for promoting positive behaviour. The structure of this book represents the process involved in developing a whole-school approach to promoting positive behaviour. The contingent link between behaviour and learning has to be established. Conceptual clarity about learning need, learning difficulty, and learning provision is imperative. The whole child becomes the focal point when her or his common, distinct and individual needs are identified and met. These needs are relative and relevant to the learning context. This book has aimed to demonstrate how the spiritual needs of all children can be met in a school setting and to assert that a child who experiences learning difficulties has the same entitlement to spiritual development as every other child.

It is important that an emphasis is placed upon the child's needs rather than their difficulties. This provides a more respectful and fruitful route into the teaching and learning process. The positive and negative factors that determine the interaction between the child, the teacher, and the learning environment have to be analysed and altered so that learning is a positive experience which increases a child's self-esteem. The process and tools of differentiation play a vital part in enabling a child to achieve success and in ensuring that the child and

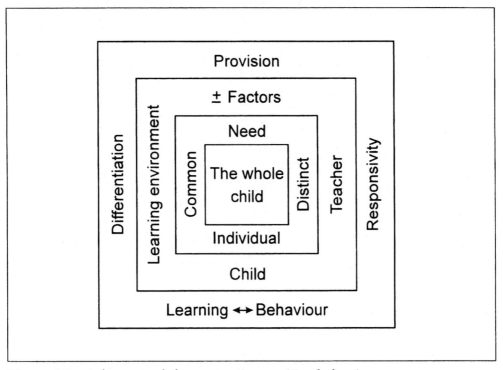

Figure 6.1   A framework for promoting positive behaviour

the teacher can learn together. Once the complex learning picture of the child has been completed, a teacher can begin to observe and analyse behaviour. Observing behaviour and analysing data is a continuous process aimed at helping the child, and the teacher, to understand and change behaviour.

It is at this point that positive approaches and strategies become successful. They take place within a planned and cohesive theoretical framework that is constructed by the learning needs of the child. The teacher in the learning zone will be preventative and responsive rather than reactive and confrontational. The latter approach provides a passport to the battle zone. In a special school the needs of the pupils will determine the needs of the staff. Review and reflection, or a similar school-based support system, can meet the needs of the staff and provide a supportive and collaborative working environment. This will improve the quality of teaching and learning.

In Figure 1.1, I emphasised how provision can meet need, ensure progress, and bridge the difficulty gap. It is not accidental that review and reflection, a manifestation of that model, takes us back to the first figure in the book. This is because the structure of the book also reflects the cyclical nature of the teaching and learning process. At the heart of a positive approach to the teaching and learning process, and at the heart of this book, is the child.

Bibliography

Ainscow, M. (1991) *Effective Schools for All*. London: David Fulton Publishers.

Ayers, H., Clarke, D. and Murray, A. (1995) *Perspectives on Behaviour: A Practical Guide to Intervention for Teachers*. London: David Fulton Publishers.

Barber, M. (1996) *The Learning Game – Arguments for an Education Revolution*. London: Victor Gollancz.

Bines, H. (1995) 'Risk, routine and reward: confronting personal and social constructs in research on Special Educational Needs', in P. Clough and L. Barton (eds) *Making Difficulties: Research and the Construction of SEN*. London: Paul Chapman.

Brown, E. (1996) *Religious Education for All*. London: David Fulton Publishers.

Byers, R. and Rose, R. (1996) *Planning the Curriculum for Pupils with Special Educational Needs: A Practical Guide*. London: David Fulton Publishers.

Carpenter, B. (1996) 'Enabling access', in B. Carpenter, R. Ashdown and K. Bovair. (eds) *Enabling Access – Effective Teaching and Learning for Pupils with Learning Difficulties*. London: David Fulton Publishers.

Carpenter, B., Ashdown, R. and Bovair, K. (eds) (1996) *Enabling Access – Effective Teaching and Learning for Pupils with Learning Difficulties*. London: David Fulton Publishers.

Carpenter, B. (1997) 'Finding the family: early intervention and the families of children with special educational needs', in B. Carpenter (ed.) *Families in Context – Emerging Trends in Family Support and Early Intervention*. London: David Fulton Publishers.

Clarke, D. and Murray, M. (1996) *Developing and Implementing a Whole-School Behaviour Policy – a Practical Approach*. London: David Fulton Publishers.

Clements, J. (1987) *Severe Learning Disability and Psychological Handicap*. Wiley: Chichester.

Cooper, P. Smith, C. and Upton, G. (1995) *Emotional and Behavioural Difficulties – Theory to Practice*. London: Routledge.

Cooper. P. (1996) 'Pupils as partners – pupils' contributions to the governance of schools', in K. Jones and T. Charlton (eds) *Overcoming Learning and Behaviour Difficulties – Partnership with Pupils*. London: Routledge.

Creese, A., Daniels, H. and Norwich, B. (1997) *Teacher Support Teams in Primary and Secondary Schools*. London: David Fulton Publishers.

Daniels, H. (1996) 'Back to basics : three 'R's for Special Needs Education', *British Journal of Special Education* 23(4), 155–61.

Department for Education (1994) *Religious Education and Collective Worship*. Circular 1/94. London: DfE.

Department for Education (1994) *The Education of Children with Emotional and Behavioural Difficulties.* Circular 9/94. London: DfE.

Department for Education and Employment (1997) *Excellence for All Children: Meeting Special Educational Needs.* London: The Stationery Office.

Department of Health (1989) *The Children Act 1989.* London: HMSO.

Department of Health (1993) *Guidance on Permissible Forms of Control in Children's Residential Care.* Department of Health Publications unit.

Department of Education and Science (1989) *Discipline in schools* (Elton Report). HMSO.

Detheridge, T. and Detheridge, M. (1997) *Literacy through Symbols.* London: David Fulton Publishers.

De Wit, T. (1994) *All together (k)now. Possibilities for Integration in Europe: Secondary Education.* Utrecht: Seminarium voor Orthopedagogiek.

Doyle, B. (1997) 'Transdisciplinary approaches to working with families', in B. Carpenter (ed.) *Families in Context – Emerging Trends in Family Support and Early Intervention.* London: David Fulton Publishers.

Durand, V. M. (1990) *Severe Behavior Problems: A Functional Communication Training Approach.* New York: Guilford Press.

Dyregrov, A. (1991) *Grief in Children: A Handbook for Adults.* London: Jessica Kingsley.

Emerson, E. (1995) *Challenging Behaviour: Analysis and Intervention in People with Learning Difficulties.* Cambridge University Press.

Eyre, D. (1997) *Able Children in Ordinary Schools.* London: David Fulton Publishers.

Farrell, P. (1995) 'Guidelines for helping children with emotional and behavioural difficulties', in P. Farrell (ed.), *Children with Emotional and Behavioural Difficulties: Strategies for Assessment and Intervention.* London: The Falmer Press.

Fish, J. (1989) *What is Special Education?* Milton Keynes: Open University Press.

Fish, J. and Evans, J. (1995) *Managing Special Education: Codes, Charters and Competition.* Milton Keynes: Open University Press.

Garner, P. and de Pear, S. (1996) 'Tales from the exclusion zone: the views of teachers and pupils', in E. Blyth and J. Miller (eds), *Exclusion from School.* London: Routledge.

Gersch, I. (1996) 'Teachers are people too!' *Support for Learning* 11(4), 165–69.

Goldthorpe, M. (1998) *Effective IEPS through Circle Time.* Cambridge: LDA.

Greenhalgh, P. (1994) *Emotional Growth and Learning.* London: Routledge.

Hargreaves, D. H., Hestor, K. H. and Mellor, J. M. (1975) *Deviance in Classrooms.* London: Routledge and Kegan Paul.

Harris, J., Cook, M. and Upton, G. (1996) *Pupils with Severe Learning Difficulties Who Present Challenging Behaviours: A Whole School Approach to Assessment and Intervention.* Kidderminster: BILD Publications.

Herbert, M. (1986) *Behavioural Treatment of Children with Problems: A Practice Manual.* London: Academic Press.

Hewett, D. and Arnett, A. (1996) 'Guidance on the use of physical force by staff in educational establishments', *British Journal of Special Education* 23(3), 130–33.

Hinchcliffe, V. (1994) 'A special special need: self advocacy, curriculum and the needs of children with severe learning difficulties', in S. Sandow (ed.) *Whose Special Need?* London: Paul Chapman.

Hitchcock, G. and Hughes, D. (1994) *Research and the Teacher: A Qualitative Introduction to School-Based Research.* London: Routledge.

Hornby, G. (1995) *Working with Parents of Children with Special Needs.* London: Cassell.

Kelly, G. (1955) *The Psychology of Personal Constructs.* New York: W. W. Norton.

Lewis, A. (1995) *Children's Understanding of Disability.* London: Routledge.

Lloyd-Smith, M. and Dwyfor Davies, J. (eds) (1995) *On The Margins: The Educational Experience of 'Problem' Pupils.* Staffordshire: Trentham.

Lynch, M. *Creation Stories.* BFSS National RE Centre. Brunel University College.

Lyon, C. (1994) *Legal Issues Arising from the Care, Control and Safety of Children with Learning Disabilities who also Present Severe Challenging Behaviour: A Guide for Parents and Carers.* London: Mental Health Foundation.

MacGilchrist, B., Mortimore, P., Savage, J. and Beresford, C. (1995) *Planning Matters : The Impact of Development Planning in Primary Schools.* London: Paul Chapman.

McGee, J. J., Menolascino, F. J., Hobbs, D. C. and Menousek, P. E. (1987) *Gentle Teaching : A Non-aversive Approach to Helping Persons with Mental Retardation.* New York: Human Sciences Press.

McManus, M. (1995) – *Troublesome Behaviour in the Classroom: Meeting Individual Needs.* (Second edition). London: Routledge.

McNamara, S. and Moreton, G. (1995) *Changing Behaviour : Teaching Children with Emotional and Behavioural Difficulties in Primary and Secondary Classrooms.* London: David Fulton Publishers.

Mittler, P. and Mittler H. (eds) (1994) *Innovations in Family Support for People with Learning Disabilities.* Chorley: Lisieux Hall.

Moseley, J. (1997) *Quality Circle Time in the Primary Classroom.* Cambridge: LDA.

Narayanasamy, A. (1997) 'Spiritual dimensions of learning disability', in B. Gates and C. Beacock *Dimensions of Learning Disability.* London: Bailliere Tindall.

National Curriculum Council (1993) *Spiritual and Moral Development : A Discussion Paper.* York: National Curriculum Council.

Nind, M. and Hewett, D. (1994) *Access to Communication: Developing the Basics of Communication with People with Severe Learning Difficulties through Intensive Interaction.* London: David Fulton Publishers.

Nolan, C. (1987) *Under the Eye of the Clock.* London: Weidenfeld and Nicolson.

Norwich, B. (1990) 'How an entitlement can become a restraint', in H. Daniels and J. Ware (eds) *Special Educational Needs and the National Curriculum. The Impact of the Education Reform Act.* London: Kogan Page.

Norwich, B. (1996) 'Special needs education: inclusive education or just education for all?' Inaugural Professorial Lecture, Institute of Education, University of London.

Norwich, B. (1997) 'Exploring the perspectives of adolescents with moderate learning difficulties on their special schooling and themselves: stigma and self-perceptions', *European Journal of Special Needs Education* 12(1), 38–53.

O'Brien, T. (1996) 'Challenging behaviour: challenging an intervention', *Support for Learning* 11(4), 162–64.

O'Brien, T. (1997) 'RE as a focus for improving teaching and learning in a special school', *REsource – The Journal of the Professional Council for Religious Education* 19(2), 3–7.

OFSTED (1997) *The Annual Report of Her Majesty's Chief Inspector of Schools: Standards and Quality in Education 1995/96.* London: HMSO.

Otto, R. (1950) *The Idea of the Holy.* Oxford: Oxford University Press.

Ouvry, C. (1987) *Educating Children with Profound Handicaps.* Kidderminster: BIMH Publications.

Ouvry, C., and Saunders, S. (1996) 'Pupils with profound and multiple learning difficulties', in B. Carpenter., R. Ashdown and K. Bovair. (eds) *Enabling Access – Effective Teaching and Learning for Pupils with Learning Difficulties.* London: David Fulton Publishers.

Park, K. (1997) 'How do objects become objects of reference? A review of the literature on objects of reference and a proposed model for the use of objects in communication', *British Journal of Special Education* **24**(3), 108–14.

Peagam, E. (1995) 'Emotional and behavioural difficulties : the primary school experience', in Farrell, P. (ed.) *Children with Emotional and Behavioural Difficulties: Strategies for Assessment and Intervention.* London: The Falmer Press.

Robson, C. (1993) *Real World Research : A Resource for Social Scientists and Practitioner Researchers.* Oxford: Blackwell.

Rogers, B. (1991) *'You Know the Fair Rule': Strategies for Making the Hard Job of Discipline in School Easier.* Pitman: London.

Russell, P. (1997) 'Don't forget us! – messages from the Mental Health Foundation Committee's Report on services for children with learning disabilities and severe challenging behaviour', *British Journal of Special Education* **24**(2), 60–65.

Sammons, P., Hillman, J. and Mortimore, P. (1996) *Key Characteristics of Effective Schools.* Ringwood: B. and MBC Distribution Services.

Sandow, S. and Garner, P. (1995) *Advocacy, Self-Advocacy and Special Needs.* London: David Fulton Publishers.

Sartre, J. P., (1943) *Being and Nothingness.* (7th reprint, 1996). London: Routledge.

SCAA Discussion Papers: No 3. (1995) *Spiritual and Moral Development.* London: School Curriculum and Assessment Authority.

SCAA (1996) *Education for Adult Life: The Spiritual and Moral Development of Young People.* London: School Curriculum and Assessment Authority.

Sebba, J., Byers, R. and Rose, R. (1995) *Redefining the Whole Curriculum for Pupils with Learning Difficulties* (revised edn). London: David Fulton Publishers.

Skinner, B. F. (1953) *Science and Human Behavior.* New York: Macmillan.

Smart, N. (1997) *Dimensions of the Sacred – An Anatomy of the World's Beliefs.* London: Harper Collins.

Sutton, R. (1991) *Assessment – a Framework for Teachers.* Windsor: NFER Nelson.

United Nations Educational, Scientific and Cultural Organisation (UNESCO) (1994) *The Salamanca Statement and Framework for Action on Special Needs Education* (adopted by the World Conference on Special Needs Education: Access and Quality. Salamanca, Spain). New York: UNESCO.

Vygotsky, L. S. (1978) *Mind in Society: the Development of Higher Psychological Processes.* Cambridge, Massachusetts: Harvard University Press.

Ware, J. (1994) 'Using interaction in the education of pupils with PMLDs (1) Creating contingency-sensitive environments', in Ware, J. (ed.) *Educating Children with Profound and Multiple Learning Difficulties.* London: David Fulton Publishers.

Ware, J. (1996) *Creating a Responsive Environment For People with Profound and Multiple Learning Difficulties.* London: David Fulton Publishers.

Wedell, K. (1990) 'Children with Special Educational Needs: past, present and future', in P. Evans and V. Varma. (eds) *Special Education: Past, Present and Future.* London: The Falmer Press.

Wedell, K. (1995) *Putting the Code of Practice into Practice : Meeting Special Educational Needs in the School and Classroom.* London: University of London Institute of Education.

Wheldall, K. and Merrett, F. (1984) *Positive Teaching : The Behavioural Approach.* London: Allen and Unwin.

Wishart, J. (1991) 'Motivational deficits and their relation to learning difficulties in young children with Down's Syndrome', in J. Watson (ed.) *Innovatory Practice and Severe*

Learning Difficulties. Edinburgh: Moray House Publications.

Wolfendale, S. (1992) *Empowering Parents and Teachers – Working for Children.* London: Cassell.

Wolfensberger, W. (1972) *The Principles of Normalisation in Human Services.* Toronto: National Institute of Mental Retardation.

Wragg, E. C., (1994) *An Introduction to Classroom Observation.* London: Routledge.

Yule, W (1991) 'Working with children following disasters', in M. Herbert. (ed.) *Clinical Child Psychology: Social Learning, Development and Behaviour.* Wiley: Chichester.

Zarkowska, E. and Clements, J. (1994) *Problem Behaviour and People with Severe Learning Difficulties: The STAR Approach.* London: Chapman Hall.

Index

Numbers in bold refer to figures and tables.

Lightning Source UK Ltd.
Milton Keynes UK
UKOW020217030412

190017UK00002B/89/A